Sew Witchy

ABOUT THE AUTHOR

Raechel Henderson (Chicago, IL) is a dual-class seamstress/shieldmaiden and a Pagan. She has been sewing professionally since 2008 and has traveled around the Midwest region selling her handmade bags, skirts, coats, and accessories at various events and conventions. She follows an eclectic and independent path, focusing on witchcraft. She currently works with Hestia and Turtle in her magickal practice, and Arachne hangs out in the window of her workroom, reminding her to check the tension on her sewing machines. She maintains a blog at idiorhythmic.com and is on Instagram and Facebook. She writes about magick, creativity, living by one's own life patterns, her family, and books.

TOOLS, TECHNIQUES & PROJECTS
FOR *Sewing Magick*

Sew *Witchy*

RAECHEL
HENDERSON

Llewellyn Publications
Woodbury, Minnesota

First Edition
First Printing, 2019

Book design by Lauryn Heineman
Charts on pages 235–38 by Raechel Henderson, created with KG-Chart for Cross Stitch © Keiji Ikuta
Cover design by Ellen Lawson
Interior illustrations by Llewellyn Art Department
Interior project photographs by Raechel Henderson except for photographs on pages iii, 9, 39, 61, 91, and 213 by Ellen Lawson
Universal Tarot by Roberto De Angelis © 2001 Lo Scarabeo. Used with permission.

Llewellyn is a registered trademark of Llewellyn Worldwide Ltd.

Library of Congress Cataloging-in-Publication Data (Pending)
ISBN: 978-0-7387-5803-9

Llewellyn Publications
A Division of Llewellyn Worldwide Ltd.
2143 Wooddale Drive
Woodbury, MN 55125-2989
www.llewellyn.com

Printed in China

CONTENTS

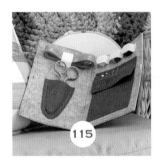

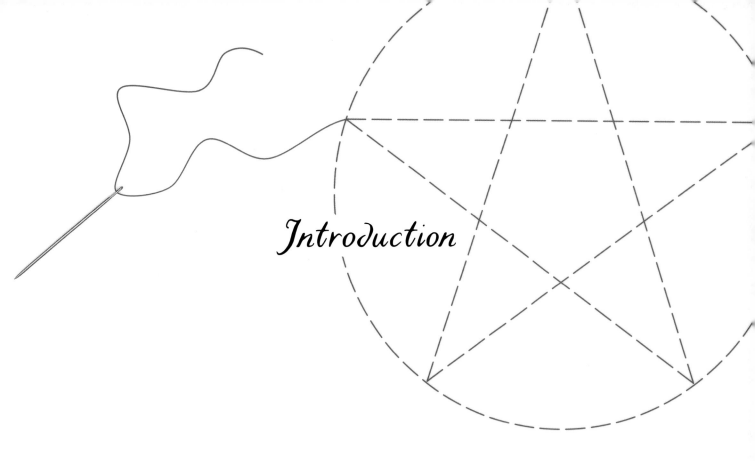

Introduction

I am both a witch and a sewist without a pedigree.

I was raised as a Baptist in the Bighorn Basin of Wyoming. I taught Vacation Bible School, attended church camp each summer, sang in the Christmas programs, and even presented the children's sermon. To be honest, though, my dedication was more to my grandmother than to the Christian God. The closest I ever came to spiritual experiences was in the woods during church camp. These feelings I kept to myself, so as not to upset her.

I was, and still am, an avid reader, and I was drawn to books that featured magic and witches. It wasn't until I came across Scott Cunningham's *Living Wicca* that I came to understand that they were real. Of course, being an introvert, and still suffering under the shameful feelings instilled by Christianity, my instruction in Paganism and magick was limited to books and websites.

With the exception of a couple of home economics classes in middle school, I am self-taught in sewing. Growing up, I made a few pillows, went through a period in high school when I made rag dolls (complete with costumes), and was conscripted into repairing torn jeans for my father. Beyond that, I didn't really sew.

The turning point came in 2004, after the birth of my daughter. I had spent my pregnancy wearing the same three pairs of sweatpants. Except, you don't go right back to your pre-pregnancy weight after you have a baby, and so I was still wearing those sweatpants. That's when I dragged out a sewing machine I hadn't used in years.

I bought fabric and a pattern with the plan to make a pair of drawstring pants. Having never used a commercial pattern, I cut and cursed and worked my way through a project that was advertised as taking one hour (it took three days). I broke needles, poked myself with pins, remembered the lesson about not using your fabric scissors on paper too late, and ripped out seams with great abandon. But, at the end of it all, I had a pair of linen pants that fit me exactly.

It was my spiritual experience.

That pair of pants opened the floodgates to making more clothing for myself. That led to sewing costumes for friends. In 2008 I found myself divorced, with a young daughter to support, and have since then made my living with my sewing skills, working on projects ranging from corsets to capes and skirts to pouches. Many of the projects in this book started out as items I made for sale.

The point of all this is that both sewing and magick can be learned and performed without the need for formal instruction from a higher authority. In fact, historically, much of sewing was done in the home, learned from a parent or older family member. Though I know several people who attended school for fashion design, pattern drafting, and so on, I know just as many talented sewists who never took a class but instead learned everything from trial and error. In between those two poles are many other people who knit, make lace, bead, mend, and engage in other arts and crafts who learned from classes, from grandmothers, and from YouTube videos and blogs.

The same goes for magick. Folk magick has a long tradition stretching back to the first time a hunter-gatherer drew an antelope on a cave wall to ensure a successful hunt. While there are several systems of magick that have been codified in books and specific religious practices, folk magick continues to flourish everywhere. Covens, high priests and priestesses, and orders offer instruction and support in spellwork. At the same time, there are a great number of solitary practitioners who get their information from the same place as self-taught sewists: books, blogs, Tumblr, and so on.

Thirteen-plus years of sewing experience and half a lifetime of practicing spellwork in some form or another are where this book comes from. I wrote down my patterns and spells to share with any sewist who has wanted to incorporate magick into their work and any witch who has wanted to try their hand at spell crafting in a more literal sense. I believe, as Pam Grossman writes in *Literary Witches*, that "weavers, potters, cooks, and healers—all have Witchly connotations, for they have traditionally been women with the gift of alchemizing something crude into something fine." In a day and age when so much emphasis is placed on credentials there is something rebellious and right about encouraging people to try an activity without a teacher looking over their shoulder. Pick up a pattern, choose some fabric, and sew that seam. And if it comes out crooked, well, that's what seam rippers are for.

WHAT'S IN THIS BOOK?

Sew Witchy is broken up into several parts: Tools, Materials, and Techniques; Correspondences and Magick; Spells and Magick; Magickal Crafts; and the appendix.

Tools, Materials, and Techniques covers the tools you'll need to get sewing. Some of the sections, such as Sewing Tools and Notions, are written with the beginning sewist in mind. The witch will find suggestions on using these notions in spellwork and ritual and suggested magickal correspondences for tools and fabric. The Techniques section is concerned with construction concepts that will be needed for making the projects. The focus here is mainly on the mundane and practical aspects of sewing.

Correspondences and Magick covers working magick into your sewing. Here concepts like number and shapes in magick, calling on deities to aid in your sewing, and how to gain a workshop helper are covered.

The next two sections go beyond theory and into the practical part of this Book of Shadows. Spells and Magick concentrates on spellwork and rituals. This is where familiar spells get a fancy-work update, such as the Witch Bottle on page 69 that makes use of spent sewing needles. Also included are ways to infuse the usually mundane tasks like preshrinking fabric or pressing seams with magickal intent. Magickal Crafts presents forty-six projects for you to make. They are grouped together by type: magickal tools, magick to wear, magick for the home, and so on. The projects range from no-sew, such as the House Gnomes on page 113, to complex, such as the Crystal/Rune Storage Bag on page 172.

At the beginning of each project you will see a list of materials needed, step-by-step instructions, and, where appropriate, a guide to charging your finished item. Many of the projects fall in between beginner and experienced levels, and the difficulty of each project is indicated by one, two, or three black scissors icons ✂, meaning beginner, intermediate, and advanced, respectively. The time it takes to complete a project from start to finish is also indicated. If a project can be machine or hand sewn, the time refers to how long it would take when machine sewing. Icons at the beginning of each project also indicate which projects can be sewn by hand 🧵 and which need a sewing machine 🪡. Most of the projects in the book can be made either way. Photos of key steps have been included with each project to aid in understanding. Each photo is marked with the number of the step to which it corresponds.

The wearables in this book were chosen specifically to be non–gender specific. As a sewist, I work with many trans and nonbinary clients. This has informed not only my sewing but also my witchcraft to be more fluid in my approach to gender. And, as one of my clients, A. C., has pointed out, "Having a majestic cloak is awesome for all genders." They are not wrong: capes, robes, cuffs, and other magickal wear are for everyone.

Finally, the appendix covers pertinent information about deities, spirit helpers, and correspondences. This is where you'll look up which colors are best to use for your current magickal project, learn about various arts and crafts deities, and find out about various workshop helpers you can call on as you sew. The patterns, embroidery designs, and cross stitch charts for the projects can be found in the Patterns section starting on page 223.

It is my hope that no matter what your level of experience in either sewing or spellworking, you'll find something of use in *Sew Witchy*. The projects and practices set down here represent my fervent belief that both sewing and witchcraft are skills that can be learned by anyone. May this book provide you with insight, inspiration, and guidance.

Blessed be.

WHAT IS MAGICK?

At its most basic, magick is the manipulation of unseen forces to achieve a desired outcome. Melanie Marquis writes in *A Witch's World of Magick*, "Emotionally charged thoughts—our intentions unleashed with will, carried by love in the pursuit of our ever-rising destinies: at its heart, this is what magick truly is." There are as many ways to accomplish this as there are Pagan paths and practices. *Sew Witchy* operates under the principle that the witch can amplify their spellcasting by surrounding themselves with crafted magickal items.

The spells and magick of *Sew Witchy* share their roots with folk magick. This is a practical approach to spell crafting. Like kitchen witchery, the process is grounded in materials on hand and spellcasting in the moment. It is as simple as charming pillow cases and sheets by embroidering them with patterns for good sleep and sweet dreams. That's not to say one can't incorporate more elaborate ceremony into the workings that follow. Quarters can be called, candles lit, bells rung, and deity invoked. Sewing spell-work can be as simple or complex as you wish. The rituals outlined in this book can be adapted as needed to better align with your personal practice.

A key component to magick is visualization. A witch can burn all the candles, collect all the crystals, intone all the chants they want, but without visualization the magick won't work. As Ann Moura writes in her book *Green Witchcraft*, "The magic comes from within the practitioner—the supplies are an aid in focusing that magic." Visualization combines your will with the magickal ingredients to bring about the result you want. The following spells and projects call on a lot of visualization. And because of the time and effort that goes into making something by hand, you are given several opportunities to do so. From selecting and preparing materials to the actual construction to the final consecration—by the time your project is ready for use, it will be saturated with your intentions and imbued with your will.

The approach to magick in this book also relies on the concept summed up in the folk etymology of the word *abracadabra*: "I say these words and so shall it be." This is the concept of the Will being the force behind the magick. Does this mean that you say, "I will win a million dollars in the lottery tomorrow," and it comes true? Well, no, it's not that simple. Otherwise, there'd be a lot more millionaires running around. Will as the force behind magick works in the same way as will as the force behind mundane tasks. If you are looking for a job, you put out résumés, you network, you dress your best for interviews. You are putting in the effort to get that job. Adding in a spell to bring job prospects your way works on the same principle: doing everything you can to make something happen, with the understanding that you are operating in a world, both seen and unseen, that is filled with the Will of others.

This formula—spell components + visualization + Will = magick—runs throughout *Sew Witchy*. It puts the majority of the work on the witch because, ultimately, magick is a tool, not a solution. A witch could perform a spell to get rid of a headache, or they could take an aspirin. Both ways might work, but one is more likely to work than the other. Approach this book with that understanding and you'll find greater success in your spellwork.

WHY SEWING MAGICK?

Fiber arts—spinning, weaving, sewing, and so on—are one of the earliest craft forms in human history. The oldest pair of footwear is over 9,000 years old and made from twined sagebrush bark found in Fort Rock Basin, Oregon. A skirt woven from reeds about 5,500 years ago was found in an Armenian cave. And the Tarkhan Dress made from linen dates over 5,000 years old. These garments are notable for having been found at all, as the materials used in their construction are susceptible to disintegration. Their existence speaks to a larger, and longer, history of clothing, purses, shoes, blankets, and more.

More recent examples of clothing and accessories from the past millennium include a number of ritual and funerary garments. These clothes, never meant for mundane wear, carry with them the mystique of the magickal in their creation. Looking beyond those items, even everyday garments made before the last century were imbued with creative energy. The work that went into making even the simplest of tunics was substantial.

Beyond clothing, sewing has been used in magick for as long as can be remembered. Spell bags and pouches litter stories throughout ancient history: from medicine bags to the bag in which Odysseus carried the winds. Embroidery was often used for magickal means, such as the needlework noted by Judika Illes in her book *Encyclopedia of 5,000 Spells*: "The exquisite traditional embroidery motifs of Baltic, Hungarian, Romany and Slav women confer blessings, power, protection and fertility."

Today, with fast fashion, free T-shirts, and bargain racks in every store, it is easy to take our clothing for granted. I've seen this attitude extend to any handmade item when vending at craft shows. There is a special kind of shopper who will dismiss a knitted scarf as too expensive. Perhaps it is a ploy to start bargaining, or perhaps the person really doesn't understand how many hours went into making it. Either way, it comes from the same place: the cheapening of not only labor but creative work. And, as annoying as this attitude might be to me, it is one that keeps millions slaving for pennies a day in sweat shops in other countries. I can ignore the rude customers, refuse to bargain, and not suffer overly for it. This is not a privilege people working in factories in India, China, and elsewhere have.

There is a flipside to this, however, a contradiction that nonetheless goes hand in hand with the dismissive attitude. Those who can craft, knit, sew, or otherwise take raw goods and turn them into something else are often valued as talented. For every person who has balked at the prices on my goods, there have been two more people who gush over the work I have done. I constantly hear, "Oh, you are so clever! So talented! I could never sew! I can't even sew a button!" The same distance that encourages us to see the price points of cheap clothing sold in big box stores as reasonable has elevated sewing to a refined space. What was once considered a necessary skill for everyone is now viewed as, well, magick.

These two sides give sewing magick a special kind of energy and tension. It is, in many ways, a subversive act, tapping into the magick that comes from doing the unexpected. As an activity that looks ordinary, it allows the secret witch to work their magick right out in the open. And again in contrast to that, its roots in group events like the quilting bee or sewing circle make it an excellent idea for coven work. In its very nature, sewing involves duality that can be leveled into all manner of spellwork.

Beyond abstract concepts, there are many other reasons to pick up needle and thread and sew yourself some magick. Silver RavenWolf writes in *HedgeWitch*, "When stitching, your mind infuses the project with your special magick with every movement of the needle. The repetitive nature of the work allows you to slip into a light, meditative state, soothing the nerves and allowing a field of harmonious opportunity wherein anything can be manifested." Working with your hands can give added "oomph" to a spell and tie you more intimately to it. Wearing something you've sewn is just like wearing a talisman you've charged during ritual. And depending on what style you choose, no one would know that the cowl neck dress you are wearing is actually charmed to bring good luck into your life. Sewing magick doesn't even require you to create a garment from scratch. Spells like the Witch Stitches on page 71 can be made with ready-made clothes you already have.

Sewing magick allows you to create complex and multilayered spellcraft through the use of color, materials, symbols, and visualization. In the appendix you'll find various correspondences that will allow you to fine-tune your creations to very specific purposes. This gives you greater control and flexibility over your magick. All the items necessary for the following spells and crafts can be picked up cheaply from craft and thrift stores, garage sales, or even various events like ZeroLandfill Chicago, where art supplies are gathered together and given away to keep them from ending up on the garbage heap.

Finally, sewing your ritual tools and garb gives you more control over what energy those items absorb. There is something special about pulling on a robe or picking up a poppet that was made by your own hands. These items are bound to you in a way store-bought items usually aren't. It also allows you to know exactly what has gone into the making of your ritual items. Whether you are dedicated to using only organic materials, have an allergy to certain fabrics, or don't want to have any synthetic materials on your altar, making your own tools allows you to be certain they satisfy your requirements.

All of the above aside, I am presuming that if you picked up this book, you are looking for a way to bring magick into your life through sewing. To that end, I say read on, and happy sewing.

GETTING STARTED

In 1949 Mary Brooks Picken wrote in the *Singer Sewing Book* the following advice:

> Prepare yourself mentally for sewing. Think about what you are going to do. . . . Never approach sewing with a sigh or lackadaisically. Good results are difficult when indifference predominates. Never try to sew with a sink full of dirty dishes or beds unmade. When there are urgent housekeeping chores, do these first so your mind is free to enjoy your sewing. . . . When you sew, make yourself as attractive as possible. . . . Have on a clean dress. . . . Keep a little bag full of French chalk near your sewing machine where you can pick it up and dust your fingers at intervals. . . . Have your hair in order, powder and lipstick put on. . . . [If] you are constantly fearful that a visitor will drop in or your husband will come home and you will not look neatly put together, you will not enjoy your sewing as you should.

I've always loved that advice—minus the outdated, patriarchal claptrap—not only because it is solid, but because it points out that sewing is serious business. And also because it is the kind of advice given for ritual work. When you are working a ritual, casting a spell, praying, collecting herbs, or what have you, there is a process of preparation, steps one follows to align their Will with their goal. We mentally prepare ourselves. We gather our materials. We cleanse ourselves and consecrate our workspace. We make sure we won't be interrupted. Readying ourselves for magick and readying ourselves for sewing follow the same steps.

To that end, I recommend taking the Singer advice as an approach to your magickal sewing projects, with the same attention to preparation, cleansing, and consecration you would use for a ritual spellcasting.

There are plenty of ways to do this, depending on your path and preferences. First, be absolutely clear on what you are going to make and what its purpose is going to be. Write it down in your Book of Shadows, plan it out on a vision board, or envision what the final project will look like and how it will be used.

Pick a time when you can work uninterrupted. For more complex projects, this will mean several sessions. Break the project into small, manageable chunks. Use sacred numbers to add resonance to these sessions (such as three one-hour or seven half-hour sessions). Or schedule time to sew on days or phases of the moon that are associated with your project's goals (see the section Magickal Timing for Sewing on page 51 for more on this). The idea is to align as many aspects as possible to your purpose to help you maintain the right state of mind, attitude, and magickal awareness.

Wash and dress yourself for sewing. This can be as complex as bathing in scented oils and donning ritual robes. Or it could be as simple as washing your hands, putting on your favorite or an appropriate scented oil, and putting on your comfy clothes. The point is that you are signaling to yourself, the mystical world, and the universe that you are going to make something magickal.

Make sure you have everything you need—tools, materials, and so on—and consecrate your work area. Call the quarters, light candles and incense, sound a bell, or just spend a few minutes in silent meditation. However your path creates sacred space, now is the time to do it.

When it is all said and done, sew. Enjoy the feeling of creation. That, in and of itself, is magickal.

When you have finished, clean your space and your head. Ground yourself. Drink some water (or wine). Just as with a magick circle, you need to disperse the energy you've raised and signal an end to the magick. Put away your tools, snuff the candles, and so on. Shift your mind from magick making and bring it back to mundane matters. All of this is as important as the preparations at the start of your sewing session.

Tools, Materials,

and Techniques

Sewing Tools and Notions

When embarking on a path of magickal sewing, you start to see everything in a new light: your sewing space, fabric choices, your tools. I have a relationship with my sewing tools, from the sewing machine named Kenny, whom I bought in 1996, to the matching set of shears and scissors I got in 2008 when I faced divorce. I feel a sense of camaraderie with them. I talk to them, envision personalities, and even occasionally curse them, but through it all I know that my tools contribute to the success or failure of my work.

Below is a list of the sewing tools and notions used throughout this book, along with information on each.

NEEDLES AND PINS

Needles and pins especially have a long history of magickal use in various paths and practices as varied as the Scandinavian folk magick called *Trolldom* and Appalachian magick. They are used in witch bottles, voodoo dolls, and protections spells.

In practical terms, the needles used in the following projects range from hand-sewing sharps and embroidery needles to machine needles. If you are new to sewing, pick up a variety of hand-sewing needles to help you find a size you are comfortable with. For machine needles, use a brand recommended by your machine's operating manual. You'll need needles that can sew regular weight fabrics as well as knits. When sewing knit fabrics on a sewing machine, make sure you use a ballpoint needle. This is made with a rounded point to slide between the fabric threads, rather than piercing them, which causes snags and curling. This isn't an issue when hand sewing and regular sharps needles can be used.

Making sure you are using the right needle for a project will make all the difference.

Sewing machine needles come in various sizes, and different manufacturers will use different systems of sizing. Whatever system a company uses, they all follow the rule that the smaller the number the finer the needle. Each company will explain which needle size is for which kind of fabric. They will also have specialty needles for certain fabric (stretch, leather, etc.) and for certain thread (metallic, embroidery, etc.).

Hand-sewing needles work on an opposite sizing guide: the larger the number the finer the needle. Hand-sewing needles come in a variety of points, as well, from sharps with sharp points and small eyes, to embroidery needles with blunt points and large eyes. Needle packages will be labeled with what kind they are and what they are used for.

Throughout *Sew Witchy,* the type of hand-sewing needle you'll need will be mentioned in the materials list. If a specialized sewing machine needle is needed for a project, that will be mentioned as well, although you will need to check with the owner's manual for your machine to find which brand of needle to get.

Straight pins come with either a metal head or colored balls made from glass or plastic. Either type is fine for sewcraft, although the ball-headed pins can be used in spellwork as you sew.

Pinhead Colors for Projects

One way to incorporate particular color energies into a project is to use pins with colored heads. Use them when pinning patterns to the fabric, and holding pieces together.

For example, for a purse, use green-headed pins to imbue it with money energies. For a gift to a friend, use pink-headed pins. Look at the appendix to find a color correspondence table to help you choose colors suited for your project.

Gather the appropriate colored pins together before working and visualize the energy that you wish to set into your project. As you use the pins, see the energy and your intentions piercing the fabric.

Pincushion

You can make the Spider Pincushion on page 106 or buy one. If you decide to buy a pincushion, make sure it has an emery filling or comes with a sharpening attachment (usually shaped as a strawberry) to keep your pins and needles sharp.

THREAD

Thread has an even wider range of use in magick than pins and needles. Many folk remedies involve using thread that had been tied around an afflicted person for diagnostic or healing purposes. Thread is used in knot magick to tie up spells for later use. The variety of colors and materials of thread available makes it one of the most useful magickal components one can use.

The most common thread is all-purpose polyester thread. If you are trying to avoid using non-natural fibers in your sewcraft, however, you can substitute it for silk or all-cotton thread. Embroidery floss is used for any projects that call for decoration, embroidery, or cross stitch. The floss comes in skeins of six threads. When using the floss, you will first cut the length you want, then separate the threads, pulling out only the number you need (usually two or three).

INTERFACING, HEM TAPE, AND WASH-AWAY STABILIZER

Heavy-weight craft interfacing is thicker than most interfacing. It is stiff and used to give structure to bags, hats, and other projects that need structural support. It is used throughout this book for various projects because it is lightweight, is flexible, and can be sewn through if needed. You will find it under a variety of names: heavy weight, craft weight, extra-firm. No matter the name, its thickness will give it away. The interfacing comes in two different styles: fusible and sew in. All projects in *Sew Witchy* use the fusible kind.

Hem tape is not tape at all. It is a thin "ribbon" of fusible interfacing meant to be used for quick hems. It comes in rolls and is placed between two pieces of fabric, which are then ironed. The heat of the iron melts the hem tape, "gluing" the fabric together.

Wash-away stabilizer is a thin, transparent film on which fabric can be sewn. It dissolves in water. Often used for embroidery designs, we'll be using it in this book for the Trickster Scarf on page 127.

TAPE MEASURE AND RULERS

Some projects will require you to take measurements. A standard tape measure will work just fine. It has the added benefit of acting a bit like a ceremonial garment. The act of draping a tape measure around your neck signals that serious sewing work is about to begin.

Quilter's rulers—usually square or rectangular and made of plastic—are useful, but not necessary, for projects like the Crystal/Rune Storage Bag on page 172.

PATTERN WEIGHTS

Pattern weights are especially useful with fabrics that can't be pinned, like pleather or vinyl. They are often used to hold the pattern in place as you trace around it right on the fabric. Or they can be used in conjunction with rotary cutters. See the Pattern Weight project on page 119 to make a set of your very own.

TRANSFER PAPER

Transfer paper is used to—you guessed it—transfer markings onto fabric. To use, you sandwich the transfer paper between your fabric and a piece of paper with the design you want to transfer. Make sure the design is face up. Secure all layers with pins around the edges. Using a ballpoint pen, trace over the design, pressing firmly but not so hard as to tear through the paper. Once you have finished, unpin the layers and remove the design and transfer papers. Your design should now be drawn on the fabric, ready for the next step.

CHALK, FABRIC PENS, AND FABRIC PENCILS

From marking magick circles to drawing sigils, chalk and other writing implements have been used in magick in innumerable ways. For the most part in *Sew Witchy*, they are used for their practical purposes: to mark designs, sewing marks, and so on. It might take some time on your part to find the type of marking tool you prefer. Currently, I am fond of a set of erasable ballpoint pens because the ink "disappears" in reaction to heat, such as that from an iron. Whatever marking tool you choose, you will need one that works on light-colored fabrics and one that works on dark-colored fabrics.

SCISSORS

Scissors are used by the Fates to cut the thread of life. They have also been used in the ancient divination art known as coscinomancy, which involves using scissors and sieves to detect a thief. Like the thread and needle, scissors are necessary for any sewing project.

In sewing, scissors aren't always scissors (an enigma which is befitting such a magickal tool). What are often called scissors are actually shears. These are scissors with a longer blade, usually 7" to 10". Other scissors include pinking shears, which have what my six-year-old son calls an "alligator mouth" that leaves a zigzag pattern as you cut. Smaller detail scissors are useful for detailed cutting work, as well as snipping threads. Some sewists also use rotary cutters.

Of the above, you'll really only need a pair of shears for the projects in *Sew Witchy*. Detail scissors are helpful but not absolutely necessary. A pair of multipurpose scissors (meaning scissors not used solely for fabric) are good to have on hand for cutting out paper patterns and interfacing.

SEAM RIPPER

Just accept right now that you will need to remove some stitches at some point in your sewing. Rather than letting this be a point of annoyance, view it as a small lesson in balance. Where there is creation, there is also destruction. In fact, I have included a spell on page 82 that uses the seam ripper. You might want to have a couple on hand as they seem to be a favorite of mischievous house gnomes, who will abscond with the seam ripper just when you need it and hide it elsewhere.

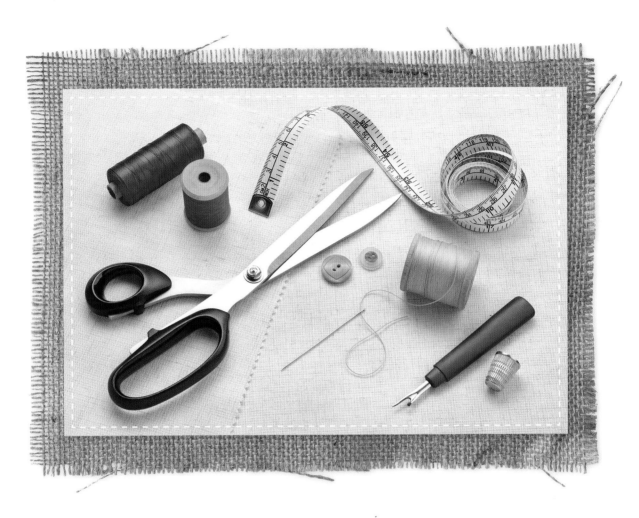

EMBROIDERY HOOP

Embroidery hoops come in various shapes and sizes, as well as materials. Pick up a couple of round wooden ones in different sizes to work the embroidery projects in *Sew Witchy*. For cross stitch projects like those on page 148 or the Protective Door Charms on page 144, you might want more hoops for display purposes.

PRESS CLOTH

A press cloth is used when ironing. It protects fabric from scorching or melting (in the case of synthetic materials) and keeps the soleplate of the iron clean. A press cloth can be as simple as a 12" × 12" piece of muslin or broadcloth. Choose a tightly woven fabric, as you don't want to press the weave of the fabric into your project.

IRON AND IRONING BOARD

Many of the projects in *Sew Witchy* require fabric to be prewashed and ironed or have steps that involve pressing. Any iron and ironing board will do. Read through the operator's manual for the iron to familiarize yourself with the various settings and what fabric they are used for. Also make sure that the iron you use has a steam setting, as that will be useful for certain projects.

STUFFING

For projects in *Sew Witchy* that require stuffing, I list polyester fiberfill in the materials list. I choose this material because it is lightweight, cheap, and commonly found where crafting supplies are sold. However, you shouldn't feel limited to polyester if you'd rather stick with all-natural fibers. There are many stuffing options, including wool and cotton fiberfill. It is simply a matter of doing a little research and asking questions of staff at stores to find the kind of stuffing you want.

You can also use scrap fabric as stuffing for some of the projects. Scrap fabric will make for a more lumpy finished project. But if you are pressed for time or money, scrap stuffing is only a pair of torn jeans or T-shirt away. When making your own stuffing, spend some time cutting the scraps into the smallest pieces possible. This will make inserting the stuffing a little easier.

BIAS BINDING

Bias binding is one of the most useful notions in the sewing basket. I have used it to face arm and neck holes in garments, to hem circle skirts and bind bibs, as straps for bags, as drawstrings for pants, as ribbon for gifts . . . and on and on and on.

What makes bias binding so useful is its stretchy nature. This feature is highlighted right in its name. The "bias" refers to when the warp and weft of a woven fabric is cut at a 45-degree angle. This gives the fabric elasticity. Bias binding comes from strips of woven fabric, usually cotton, cut on the bias and then folded to make either single or double folds. Its stretchy nature allows it to be shaped in ways that fabric cut with the grain can't.

SEWING MACHINE

While a sewing machine will make quick work of the projects in this book, it isn't necessary. Nearly all the projects in this book can be sewn by hand. However, if you don't have sewing machine and decide to get one, here are some things to keep in mind:

1   Look for a good basic sewing machine for your first purchase. None of the projects in this book require more than a straight and zigzag stitch, and most sewing doesn't require bells and whistles. Once you've gotten a few projects under your belt, you'll have a better understanding of what other attachments or stitches you'd like for future sewing.

2   Do your research before you settle on a certain machine. There are hundreds of forums online where people talk about what machines they have and use, why they bought the machine they did, and what advice they have. Talk to the people who work at your local hobby store and with people you know who sew. Oftentimes they can give you insights into what to look for.

3   You don't have to invest a ton of money into a sewing machine. Look in second-hand stores or online for machines. Oftentimes you can find a used machine that is selling for a fraction of what a new one would cost. (I experienced this when I bought an embroidery machine. A year after purchasing it, I realized that I didn't use it much and ended up selling it on Craigslist for a third of what I paid for it.) If you buy used, make sure that the machine has all the attachments, feet, and so on as well as the owner's manual. If it is missing any of these, you might want to pass on it, or you might be able to track down replacements online.

4   Machines from hobby centers might come with sewing lessons. When I bought my serger, it came with three free lessons from the vendor representative who taught the classes in the store. Local recreation centers, libraries, and colleges often have basic sewing classes as well that can give you a good basic education on how to use your machine. There is also a thriving video culture on YouTube dedicated to every aspect of sewing with particular machines. Search for the particular brand and model of your sewing machine and see if anyone has posted instructional videos for it.

5   Read the manual that comes with the machine. Play around with it, sewing practice seams on various types of fabric to get a sense of how it works. Practice threading the machine, inserting the bobbin, swapping out presser feet, and threading the needle. This will give you a chance to discover your machine's personality and quirks. You might even find yourself naming your machine, as I have: Kenny the Kenmore and Sergei the serger. (I name everything: my machines, computers, car, children, etc.)

Unusual Sewing Tools

The crafty witch knows that sometimes you have to think outside the sewing basket when it comes to tools. It doesn't matter if the tool comes from the craft store or the office supply store; what matters is that is works. To that end, here is a small list of items I find useful in my sewing that you won't find in the notions aisle:

Binder Clips: I use these when I can't use pins to clip together thick pieces of fabric.

Chopsticks: I use these when I am turning a project right-side out, especially for corners.

Wooden Skewers: Sometimes you can't or don't want to mark your fabric. In this case, you can use a wooden skewer to score your fabric. You can also use bone scoring tools that are used in paper crafts.

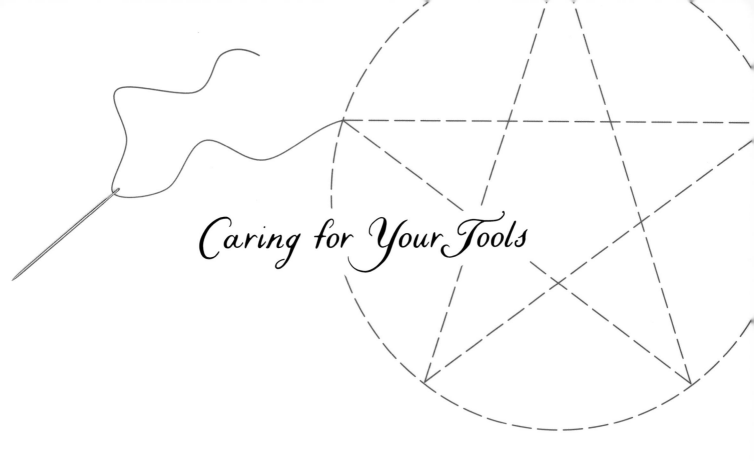

Caring for Your Tools

Magickal sewing tools are different from ceremonial or ritual tools. The athame, sword, wand, and so on may never be used in a way that would dull their edges or cause damage. Contrarily, shears, needles, irons, and sewing machines are all meant to be put to work in spellcraft. It is, therefore, important to take care of your tools. This means reading operating manuals and following suggested maintenance.

Maintenance tasks can be done as a matter of cleansing and charging your tools. After cleaning and oiling your sewing machine, you can anoint it with an oil suited to your current or next project. I have, when faced with a large project, gone so far as to mark my sewing machines with runes using washable markers. Bind runes for success, for inspiration, for completion, or any number of other intentions can be easily marked in a place where you can see them as you work. When you are no longer in need of the energy from the runes, simply wipe them away with a damp cloth.

Blades should be regularly sharpened. Some hobby and craft stores offer a sharpening service or host someone who comes in on a regular schedule to do the same. There are several sharpening tools you can also buy to use at home. I have a small sharpening tool that looks like an orange egg and has served me well for years.

Keep pins and needles sharp by using a pincushion with a filling of crushed walnut shells or emery. Pins and needles belong to the element of earth, the domain of security. As wool is associated with protective energies (see Fabric on page 23) and the lanolin in wool is thought to coat needles and pins, making them glide more easily into fabric, having a pincushion made from wool and filled with emery makes the perfect home for these most useful tools.

Just as you wouldn't leave your ritual tools out on the kitchen counter when not in use, have a place for each of your sewing tools, whether it be a sewing basket, desk drawer, or shoe box. Whatever you use, make sure all your implements go back into storage when you aren't using them. Not only will that keep you from losing them, but it will cut down on the possibility of your expensive sewing shears being used to open a bag of chips in the kitchen. You can ward your storage against intruders by holding your hands over it, palms down, and saying,

> *In this box [or drawer, basket, etc.] my tools to keep,*
> *No unauthorized soul can into creep.*
> *By water and earth and air and fire,*
> *They will face consequences most dire.*

Visualize red protective light, like flames, flowing from your palms over the storage. See anyone who rifles through it without your express permission feeling uncomfortably hot, as if they are touching something that burns, and then fleeing.

You can build on this protective magick by anointing your storage with protective oils made from herbs such as cedar, dragon's blood, sage, thistle, or any number of others. Add bind runes, protective sigils, even a sign saying, "These belong to a witch who will be very displeased if you use them without permission." You know your situation and how best to keep untrained hands off of your tools.

MAGICKAL TIMING FOR TOOL MAINTENANCE

I have a long-standing appointment in my calendar: every Sunday I clean and oil my sewing machines. The timing is purely practical: Sundays are normally idle for me. Taking care of my machines on Sunday means they are ready for work come Monday. Sunday is also recognized as the day to work on success, magickally speaking, and so the timing works out well.

You may want to time your tool maintenance on a more magickal schedule, however. If you are starting a project with a particular intent or goal, or if you want to channel certain energies into your tools, you can do so. There are books and websites that chart out magickal correspondences for months, phases of the moon, days of the week, and even hours of the day. With all that information, you can time the sharpening of your scissors to the most auspicious moment. The important thing to keep in mind, however, is to do what works for you. Some witches find that scheduled rituals aid in their magick. Some ignore astrological correspondences and perform magick whenever they feel the need. Many more fall somewhere in between. Following your own path will yield better results every time.

With regard to moon phases, the following are good guidelines:

Clean, consecrate, and charge tools on the **new or waxing moon.**

Sharpen needles, pins, and cutting tools on the **waxing moon** to banish dullness from your work.

Bless and charge tools by bathing them in moonlight during the **full moon.**

Let tools, and yourself, rest on the **dark of the moon,** the time before the crescent moon appears.

How to Clean Your Steam Iron

Using tap water in your steam iron can lead to clogged steam vents as mineral deposits are left behind. To clear the steam vents, do the following:

1 Mix a paste of 2 parts baking soda and 1 part water.

2 Spread this paste onto the soleplate of your iron and let it sit for a couple of minutes.

3 Wipe the paste off with a damp, soft cloth. (I use a cloth taken from a T-shirt my son grew out of.)

4 Use a cotton swab to clean out the steam holes.

5 Next fill the reservoir with 1 part distilled water and 1 part distilled white vinegar.

6 Turn the iron to its highest setting and turn on the steam.

7 Iron a towel or other clean piece of cloth until the reservoir is empty.

8 Refill the reservoir with clean water and let it steam again to clear out any lingering vinegar.

9 Use a dry, clean rag to wipe down the soleplate a final time.

ALL YOU NEED TO CLEAN YOUR IRON CAN BE FOUND IN YOUR KITCHEN PANTRY.

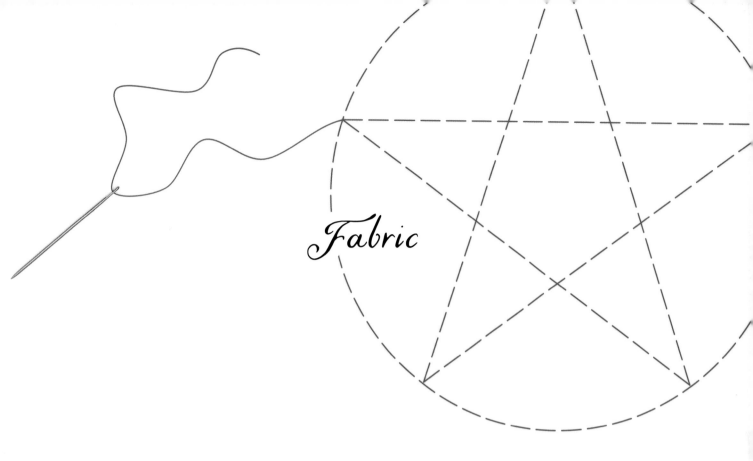

Fabric

I recommend using natural fabrics for many of the projects in this book, especially for pouches. Cotton, linen, silk, wool, and other fabrics from nature can be more easily charged for your purposes. Cotton especially comes in a range of qualities and prices to suit most any project. However, this is not a hard-and-fast rule. Even man-made materials come from components gotten from the natural world.

Do your own research, journey, or ask your magickal helpers, and make up your own mind about whether synthetics belong in your practice. If all you have on hand is some black polyester and you need to make a rune pouch, go ahead. Or if you find a rayon blend that is perfect for a project and speaks to you, go for it.

The witch learns to be flexible, as does the sewist. There will be times when you will gather all your materials and tools ahead of time, paying attention to make everything perfect. And there will be times when you will have to wing it. Everything in this book is meant to be a focus for your intentions. If you feel what you have is working for you, then it will. As Melanie Marquis points out in her book *A Witch's World of Magick*, "Basically, if you can't make magick *without* tools, you can't make magick *with* tools, either."

For projects that might be laundered (such as altar cloths), preshrink any fabric before you work with it. This will save you headaches down the line. Wash and dry the fabric and then press according to the manufacturer's instructions.

FABRIC MAGICKAL PROPERTIES

Unlike herbs, stones, colors, feathers, shells, and nearly every other magickal component under the sun, very little has been written about the magickal properties of various fabrics. Since fabric and fibers are separated from their origin, spun, and woven, it stands to reason that their energies will be a bit flexible, allowing them to be suited to a greater range of spells and rituals. With that in mind, I offer some notes on the four most popular and available natural cloths. As with everything else in this book, use your own instincts and feelings to decide if the correspondences ring true to you.

Cotton

Cotton fabric is made from the boll of the cotton plant. The fibers are plucked, mixed, beaten in cylinders, carded, drawn, roved, and then spun into thread. As such, it shares some of the qualities of the plant from which it comes: it is associated with the earth element, and it can be used magickally in spells of healing, luck, and protection. According to Cunningham, "Cotton is the best kind of cloth (next to wool) to use for making sachets, or for any time cloth is needed in magic."

One type of cotton fabric, muslin, was once a fabric highly prized in its native India and throughout the rest of the world. In her book, *Muslin*, Sonia Ashmore writes, "Muslin is an open-textured cloth, thin and sheer, woven to varying degrees of fineness depending on the quality of yarn used and the skills of both the spinner and the weaver. The surface, particularly of hand-woven muslin, has a softness to the touch that has been described as 'mossiness.'" This description of its "mossiness" along with its origin of the cotton plant reinforces cotton's place in earth's elemental realm.

In the past cotton was used as an offering. Cotton is associated with healing, as well as good luck and repelling negativity. As such it is useful for healing and luck charms. Use cotton fabric for any project, from robes to altar cloths to spell bags. It is well suited for spell bags, as it is breathable, allowing the magick to flow in and out of the pouch.

Quilting cottons especially lend themselves to magickal projects. Any Pagan symbol, from the overt to the subtle, can be found somewhere.

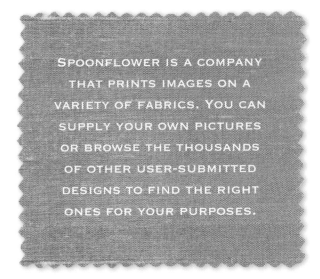

SPOONFLOWER IS A COMPANY THAT PRINTS IMAGES ON A VARIETY OF FABRICS. YOU CAN SUPPLY YOUR OWN PICTURES OR BROWSE THE THOUSANDS OF OTHER USER-SUBMITTED DESIGNS TO FIND THE RIGHT ONES FOR YOUR PURPOSES.

Linen

Linen is created from flax, a laborious process that includes "retting," or fermentation in water. Because of this and its water-absorption properties, it is associated with the water element. It is a fabric that suggests purity and wealth. As it was historically used for bedding, linen is used in many healing spells. One such spell involves tying a strip of linen from a sick person's bed to a tree. As the elements destroy the strip, the illness will be similarly destroyed in the patient.

Linen is associated with the goddess Hulda through its flaxen origin. It is used in spells of beauty, healing, money, protection, and psychic powers. Linen is especially well suited for robes and other magickal attire. Flax seeds are said to have the magickal properties of protection, abundance, and healing, and so linen inherits those properties.

While pure linen is expensive, there are several linen-like synthetics available at a lesser price point. These can be used in place of the authentic fiber. These faux fabrics require less ironing than pure linen, meaning they can be preferable for garments.

Use linen in spell bags for wealth or protection. Its association with and use for years as bedclothes points to its usefulness in dream pillows.

Silk

Silk is made from the cocoons of silkmoth caterpillars. The cocoons are soaked in hot water from which loose fibers are collected and then twisted into thread for weaving. As a fabric, it is seen as a luxurious and sought-after material for garments. Magickally, silk is considered to deflect magick and to protect the magickal energies and contents inside it, making it especially useful for tarot, rune, and crystal bags.

Caterpillars, moths, and butterflies, as well as their cocoons, represent transformation, thus making silk suited for spells and magick with regard to change, movement, and growth. Because of its association with wealth, luxury, and prestige, silk is a good fabric to use in money and prosperity spells. Use silk for tarot bags or to hold other divination tools. Silks flowers can be used as altar decorations when real flowers are unavailable.

Silk is associated with the element of air due to its airy quality and its origin. Because of its great rate of shrinkage and loss of strength when wet, it may not be suited for spells or rituals involving the water element.

Wool

Wool sheared from sheep is bathed in a chemical bath, mixed, spun, washed, and pressed to felt it. It is known for its imperviousness to cold and is often used for clothing meant to protect from cold weather. Coming from sheep, it is associated with the astrological sign Aries and the planet Mars. All these properties align it with the fire element.

Wool is associated with protection and comfort. It can be used in protective, prosperity, and healing spells. Wool felt is useful for crafts from poppets to altar decorations. Wool suiting is useful for ritual cloaks, which will keep you warm during outdoor rituals.

Cut edges of wool don't unravel, making it useful for quick circle pouches or for when you don't have time for finishing edges in a project. And though expensive, wool is a durable fiber that will last a long time, making it a worthwhile investment for spell and ritual tools.

Wool was believed to possess medicinal properties, making it suitable for healing spell bags. Felt has been used by nomadic societies for centuries in making protective amulets. When buying felt for magickal purposes, avoid the felt squares sold in hobby shops. These are petroleum-based products without even a whisper of wool. Instead look in the fabric aisle, where wool and wool-blend felts can be found. The fiber content will be listed on the cardboard bolt the felt is wrapped around.

Other Materials

Fabric made from hemp can be used in spells and projects meant to attract love, enhance psychic abilities, deepen meditation, or heal body-mind connections. Hemp cording can be especially useful for witch cords.

Plarn is yarn made from plastic bags. While it is a completely man-made material, it can still be used for sewing spellcraft. Use it for spells that require plastic's malleability and shape-shifting properties.

Leather and fur carry the magickal properties of the animal they come from. If you are a witch who is looking to avoid materials from animals, look into faux leather made from mushrooms or other plant material.

RIGHT AND WRONG SIDES OF FABRIC

Throughout the book I'll reference the "right" and "wrong" sides of fabric. This is not a question of the morality of the fabric but instead a differentiation of the outside and inside of the fabric as it was woven. The side facing out from the loom is the "right" side. In printed fabrics it will be the more brightly colored side. On fabrics like brocades one side will be patterned and the other side will have stripes of color. If you are using a solid color cloth like cotton or linen, there is often little or no difference between the two sides. When a project's instructions tell you to have fabric "right sides together," this means the printed/colorful/outside sides should be facing each other. The opposite is true if the instructions call for "wrong sides together."

FABRIC SIZES

Most fabric comes in two different widths: 44" wide and 60" wide. Most cottons come in the 44" wide, with muslin coming also in 36", 90", and even 118" wide. Most apparel fabrics and linings, as well as home décor fabrics, come in widths of 60". Widths will be marked on the end of the cardboard the fabric is wrapped around.

Fat Quarter

A special type of fabric size is called a fat quarter. Often used in quilting, the fat quarter is a precut length of cotton. It is a rectangle that is 18" long and 22" wide. It is called a fat quarter because it is a quarter of a yard; however, the way it is cut is different from what you would get if you asked for a quarter of fabric at the cutting counter (the dimensions of that cut would be 9" long by 44" wide). You can usually find fat quarters sold on their own at hobby shops.

Personalize your embroidery spellwork by combining hairs (your own or those of the spell's target) with thread in embroidered spells for protection and healing.

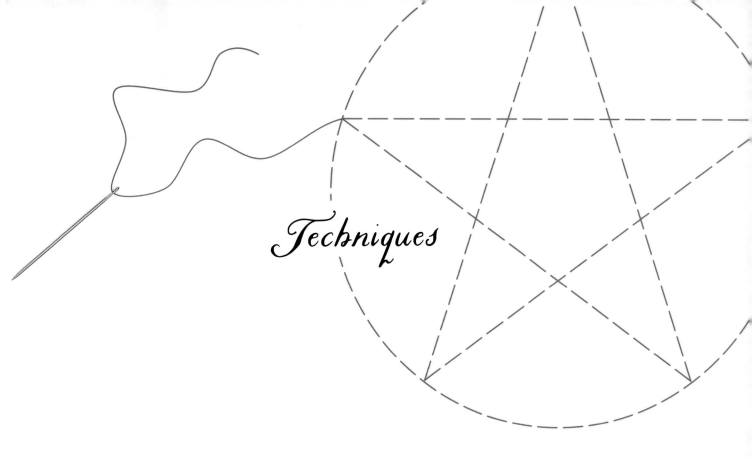

Techniques

Throughout this book there will be certain techniques and concepts mentioned. If you are a beginning sewist, some of the ideas might be unfamiliar. Here are some definitions and advice you can refer back to as you work through the projects in the book.

SEWING STITCHES

Several types of stitches are used throughout the book. These are stitches that can be done either on a sewing machine or by hand, unless noted. When working the stitches by hand, you'll knot the thread and start the stitch by pulling the threaded needle through the fabric until the knot rests against the fabric. Continue stitching by pulling the thread and needle all the way out of the fabric before inserting the needle into the fabric for the next stitch. When you have come to the end of the stitching, tie off the thread and then trim any excess.

The following are descriptions of each stitch and how to make them.

Basting Stitch

A basting stitch is a line of long stitches run in and out of a piece of fabric or multiple pieces of fabric. It is used to keep things in place for sewing. It is also used to gather fabric. On a sewing machine, use the longest stitch setting on your stitch selector (consult the owner's manual of your machine to find where this is and how to use it). When hand sewing, run the threaded needle in and out of the fabric, making stitches that are about ½" or longer.

Whip Stitch

This stitch is done only by hand and is used to join pieces of fabric together. The whip stitch is used in the book on projects that involve felt. To work it, insert the needle at the back side of two pieces you are joining together (A). Pull it through to the front then bring it around again to the back a small distance from where you first inserted the needle (B). Pull the thread through until it has wrapped around the edge. Repeat until you have completed the seam.

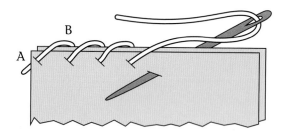

Topstitching

Topstitching, also referred to as edge stitching, is a stitch used to finish projects. This stitch not only gives a finished edge a smart appearance, but it can also serve a secondary role in closing the gap used to turn a project right-side out. To work, stitch a row of small stitches ⅛" from the finished edge of a project.

Zigzag Stitch

Zigzagging is a stitch used for decorative applications, such as on the edges of appliqués, and on the seams of knit fabrics so the thread will stretch with the fabric and not break. On a sewing machine use a zigzag stitch and presser foot (consult the owner's manual of your machine to find how to set the zigzag stitch and which presser foot is recommended for zigzag stitches). If sewing by hand, the zigzag stitch looks more like a series of slanted lines than a true zigzag.

Work this stitch by hand in this way: Bring a threaded needle through the back of the fabric (A). Insert the needle back into the fabric ¼" up from point A and pull through B. Bring the needle back through point A and pull through; this will create a vertical stitch on each side of the fabric. Next insert the needle through to the front of the fabric ¼" away horizontally from point B. This is point C. Bring the needle back again ¼" vertically from point C. This is point D. Insert the needle back into point

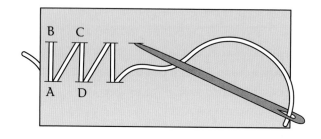

C and pull the thread through to make another vertical stitch. Bring the needle up through point D and insert it into the fabric another ¼" horizontally from point C. Continue with this stitching for the remainder of the seam.

Backstitching

Backstitching as used in this book refers to stitching backward at the start of the seam to secure the stitching. To do this on a sewing machine, start stitching, making three or four stitches. Then reverse your machine to sew backward over what you just stitched. Set your machine back to forward stitching and continue your seam. When you reach the end of your seam, repeat the backstitching to secure the seam. Consult the operator's manual for your machine to find out how to set reverse. In hand sewing the process is similar: make a few stitches and then go back over them before continuing the seam.

Slip Stitching

Slip stitching is used in this book to close turned openings where you don't want the stitches to show. This is a stitch sewn solely by hand. Work the stitch this way: Starting at one end of the turned opening, bring your needle up and through the seam allowance close to the stitching (A). Insert the needle into the opposite side directly across from point A. This is point B. Bring the needle back up a scant ⅛" from point B. This is point C. Cross over to the opposite side, directly across from point C, and insert the needle into the fabric. Continue this way until you have reached the end of the gap. Pull on the thread end to pull the gap closed.

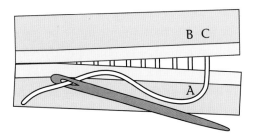

Tacking

Tacking is a quick stitch meant to hold two things together temporarily until they are sewn together. It is a stitch usually sewn by hand. To work the stitch, make three or four stitches and tie off the thread.

EMBROIDERY STITCHES

With the exception of the cross stitch designs, all the embroidery designs in this book are provided without instructions for which stitch you should use. Embroidery stitches are worked with two threads of embroidery floss for cross stitches or four threads for the chain, split, and stem stitches. The designs can be embroidered with whatever stitch you feel most comfortable with or prefer. The following is a brief overview of some stitches and how they can be used in your magickal sewing practice.

Chain Stitch

Use the chain stitch for projects that are to be long lasting, for protective spells, and for spells related to earth energy. Work the chain stitch as follows: Bring your needle up from the back of the fabric (A). Insert the needle a small distance away (B) and pull it through to make a stitch. Bring the needle back up a small distance from B. Run the needle under the A-B stitch and bring it back down into the place it came up at (C). This is your first chain. Bring the needle up another small distance away from C and run it under the first chain. Bring it back down into the place it came up at. Continue until you finish your stitching, then bring the needle back to the wrong side of the fabric, knot the thread, and trim off any excess.

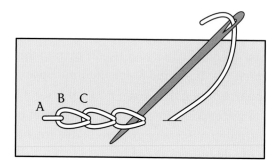

Split Stitch

The split stitch is used for projects that are meant to be disruptive: breaking habits, banishing spells, and spells that need to be done quickly. Work the split stitch as follows: Bring the needle up from the back side of the fabric (A). Insert it into the fabric a short distance from where it came up (B). Bring the needle back up in between points A and B, coming up between the threads of the stitch (C). This is where the stitch gets its name, as you are splitting the stitch. Insert the needle into the fabric a short distance from C. Bring the needle back up in between the points B and C, coming up between the threads of the stitch. Continue until you finish your stitching, then bring the needle back to the wrong side of the fabric, knot the thread, and trim off any excess.

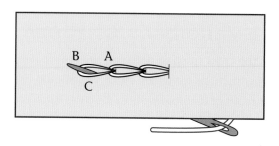

Stem Stitch

Use the stem stitch for spells that are meant to increase prosperity, health, and luck, as the stitch that follows reinforces and builds on the previous one. Work the stem stitch as follows: Bring the needle up from the back side of the fabric (A). Insert it into the fabric a short distance from where it came up (B). Bring the needle back up between points A and B to the left of the thread (C). Insert the needle into the fabric a short distance from C. Bring the needle back up in between the points B and C, again to the left of the thread. Continue until you finish your stitching, then bring the needle back to the wrong side of the fabric, knot the thread, and trim off any excess.

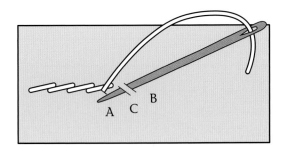

Satin Stitch

Use this stitch for glamour spells, spells that are intended to cover or obscure something, or protection spells. Satin stitching is often used to cover large portions of needlework in flat stitches. It is also used to cover the unfinished edges of appliqués. Work satin stitches for appliqué as follows: Bring the needle up from the back side of the fabric close to the unfinished edge of the appliqué (A). Insert the needle a short distance away from A in the fabric the appliqué has been attached to. This is point B. Bring the needle up again next to point A. Insert the needle next to point B. Continue this way, laying the stitches close to each other around the entirety of the appliqué. When you have finished, bring the thread to the back side of the fabric and knot it. Cut off any excess thread.

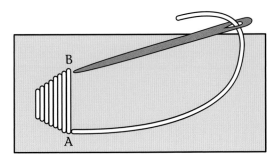

Cross Stitch

The cross stitch is for spells that require a lot of visualization and for spells that benefit from repetition. Cross stitch is often worked on Aida cloth, an open-weave cotton cloth.

The mesh provides evenly spaced holes to aid in making uniform stitches. The cross stitch looks just like it is called: a series of crosses that are stitched to make images, letters, and numbers. Cross stitch is often worked following a chart that shows what colored thread to use and where.

Work the cross stitch as follows: Bring the needle up from the back side of the fabric (A). Insert the needle into the fabric diagonally from A on the next row down of holes (B). Bring the needle back up from the back of the fabric in a hole one row above B. Insert the needle back into the fabric in a hole that is directly below A, forming a cross. This is your first stitch. Continue to make cross stitches as the chart shows you. When you have finished your stitching, knot your thread at the back of the fabric and trim off any excess.

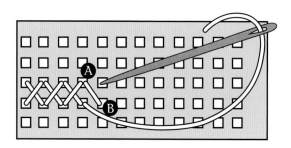

Back Stitching

Use back stitching for single-purpose spells that need to be done quickly and for spells that require a straightforward result. Unlike the backstitching outlined earlier in the Sewing Stitches section, the embroidery back stitch is used to outline or emphasize stitches and areas or as a decorative stitch on its own. Embroidery back stitching is often worked with only one strand of embroidery floss. Work the back stitch as follows: Bring the needle up from the back of the fabric at point A. Insert the needle into the fabric one hole to the right of point A. This is point B. Bring the needle up from the back of the cloth one hole to the left of point A (C) and back into the fabric at point A. Bring the needle up from the back of the cloth two holes to the left of point A. Insert the needle into point C. Continue working the stitches this way according to the charted design you are working on. When you have finished, knot your thread at the back of the fabric and trim off any excess.

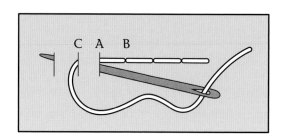

HEMS

To hem a project means to finish the unfinished edges of the fabric. This can be done either by hand or with a sewing machine. Below are two hems that are used throughout the book.

Standard Hem

The unfinished edges of altar cloths, capes, sleeve openings, and other large projects can be finished with a standard hem. To make a standard hem, do the following:

1   Turn the fabric so that the wrong side is facing up or out.

2   Fold the unfinished edge of the fabric up by ½". Press. Fold the edge another ½". Press.

3   Topstitch close to the inside edge of the hem.

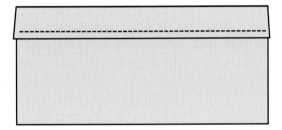

Narrow Hem

A narrow hem is a small hem used to finish the edges of small projects or for sewing detailed areas (like the neck opening in the Ritual Robe on page 133). To give a project a narrow hem, do the following:

1   Turn the fabric so that the back or wrong side is facing up.

2   Fold the unfinished edge of the fabric up by ¼". Press. Fold the edge another ¼". Press.

3   Topstitch close to the inside edge of the hem.

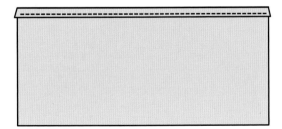

TRIMMING

Trimming Corners

After you sew a project that has corners, you will need to cut across them to reduce bulk once the project is turned. Do so by cutting 45 degrees across the corner, removing the tip, and making sure not to cut the stitching.

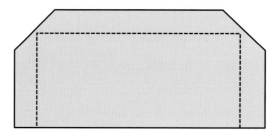

Trimming Seams

You can reduce the bulk of projects by trimming the excess fabric in the seam allowances. Use small detail scissors for the work and cut close to, but not into, the seam.

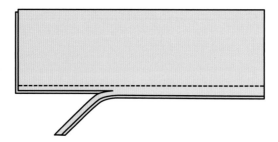

Clipping Curves

Clipping the curves in sewing helps fabric lie flat and smooth when it has been turned. After you sew a curved seam, clip the seam allowance at ½" intervals along the curve, making sure not to cut through the stitching.

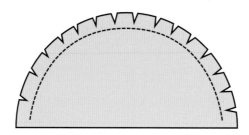

HOW TO DISPLAY YOUR SPELLWORK

Many of the projects in *Sew Witchy* are meant to be displayed, most often hung on walls (for example, the Cross Stitch Projects on page 148). You can display them a number of ways, the simplest being to frame them.

If you decide to frame a piece of sewing spellwork, consider the following advice:

For frames with glass, make sure to mat the needlework. Glass can rub against the stitching or trap moisture that will harm the fabric. Adding a mat will allow some airflow and keep the needlework friction free.

For projects that send energies out (prosperity embroidery, for example), ditch the glass of the frame and instead add some polyester fiberfill behind the fabric so that it takes a three-dimensional appearance. This gives an added boost to your magick, as it now literally bursts out into the world.

Witch Ladders like the one described on page 208 can be hung from the ceiling. Make sure they are set away from walls, shelves, and anything else that might touch them and interrupt the flow of their magick.

Charms can be displayed in an embroidery hoop rather than a frame. If you decide to use an embroidery hoop, finish the back as follows:

1   Center the design in the hoop, allowing excess fabric to hang out the back.

2   Using a basting stitch, gather up the excess fabric. Tie off the ends of the thread and push the excess fabric into the hoop. Start and end your basting stitch on the same side of the fabric to make tying the thread off easier.

3   Cut a piece of felt the same size as the embroidery hoop. Set the felt over the back, covering the excess fabric.

4   Using a whip stitch, stitch the felt to the excess fabric, covering the back of the embroidery hoop.

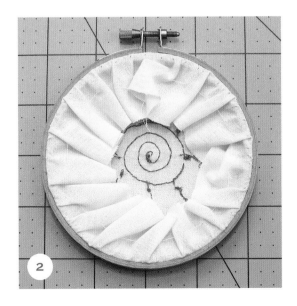

Work from the outside of the felt to make the sewing easier.

Correspondences

and Magick

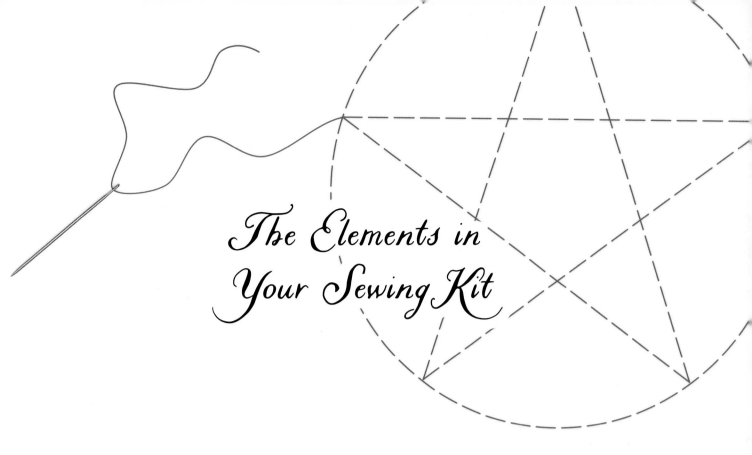

The Elements in Your Sewing Kit

There is a tendency in many modern magick traditions to categorize colors, gemstones, elements, and even feathers and shells into correspondences, listing the powers, spheres of influences, energies, and such of each. The drawback of these standardized lists is that symbols aren't universal. Additionally, these lists are often limited in scope: focusing on European trees and herbs, for example, which leaves a whole world of flora unrepresented. With the exception of the appropriation of some symbolism from various Native American tribes, this gives the impression that witchcraft is the domain of one small part of the world.

With the above in mind, treat the information that follows in this book as suggestions. My categories with regard to various sewing tools and materials is based on my own research. The lists of correspondences throughout the book have been put together from a variety of sources, with the intention of providing symbols and interpretations from a variety of magick traditions from all over the world.

Many *materia magica*—spell components—share correspondences. In those cases, when choosing a color, herb, or gemstone for your project, look at its other properties to decide. Yellow and pink, for instance, both have ties to inspiration. Yellow also has ties to persuasion, mental alertness, and creativity, while pink has ties to love, domestic harmony, and friendship. If you are looking for a color for a schoolbag, you might choose yellow, whereas if you are making a gift for a friend, you might choose pink.

Magick is a highly personal pursuit. Symbols that are meaningful to you will always be more powerful in your rituals. Take what resonates with you from this book and leave the rest behind.

EARTH

Earth is associated with the direction of north, home, security, and fertility. As such, all needles, pins, and pinning tools fall under earth's domain. This includes thread, thimbles, needle threaders, bodkins, and pincushions, as well as fabric glue and hem tape. Any sewing tool or notion that holds things together: safety pins, upholstery tacks and staples, snaps and buttons (if used as closures rather than solely for embellishment), zippers, hooks and eyes, and so on beong to earth. Pattern weights also carry earth properties.

AIR

Air is associated with the direction of east and is the domain of communication, new beginnings, and new growth. A project begins with an idea, a pattern, the taking of measurements. All measuring tools and rulers, including hem gauges, belong to the element of air and the inspiration it brings. Templates fall into this category for their association with patterns and measurements. Patterns and pattern paper correspond with the air element. Additionally, pincushions belong to air if they have emery or other pin-sharpening stuffing, as they keep pins and needles sharp. Scissor sharpeners belong to air for the same reason.

FIRE

Fire is associated with the direction of south and is the domain of energy, passion, and creativity. The spark of inspiration fans the flames of creativity to bring designs to life. Tools that transform ideas into reality fall under fire's purview: marking tools like chalk, fabric pens, and pencils, as well as tracing wheels and tracing paper. Bone folders and scoring tools also belong to fire. Even tailor tacks, those bits of thread used to mark points on garments, are included.

WATER

Water is associated with the direction of west and is the domain of emotion, the psyche, and movement. Sewing is far from a static activity—from the back and forth of the shuttle in the weaver's loom to the in-and-out motion of the sewing machine, movement is required. Therefore, all cutting tools fall under its sway: all scissors, shears, rotary cutters, X-Acto knives, seam rippers, and cutting mats. Scissors cut to the heart of the matter, and many superstitions and folk wisdom link them to emotions both positive and negative.

SPIRIT

A fifth element—spirit—is recognized by some traditions. It is associated with the center of all things. It is the realm of creativity, individuality, and enlightenment and is the seat of one's own power. To this domain belong all embellishment items: beads, cording, piping, ribbon, and floss. Embroidery hoops provide the boundaries for your work, a practical and physical circle in which to make magick. Buttons, when added for purely aesthetic reasons—rather than functional ones—add the energies of their color and materials to your work. Lace touches upon beauty for beauty's sake.

Shapes, Numbers, and Magickal Alphabets

*N*umbers and shapes are another example of how the witch can add layers of magick to their sewing spellcraft. The number of times you knot your thread can be changed to invoke certain number energies. The shapes you use in your quilts can impart grounding, fertility, or active energies. Use two threads of floss for projects in which you want balance or to invoke the god and goddess. Embroider flowers with five petals for projects that are meant to bring about change. Below is a quick overview of how to use shapes, numbers, and letters in spellwork. However, don't feel limited to these examples. If you have personal associations with certain numbers, shapes, and alphabets, use them to apply a personal touch to your project.

SHAPES

Circle

The circle is a universal symbol found in magickal practices everywhere. It represents unity, the whole, the entirety, and deity. It's no wonder that the circle shows up in designs of all types. You can use this to your advantage by mounting designs in round frames, finishing them as circle pouches, and appliquéing them as circles on quilts, cloaks, and so on. Use circular designs to bring spells to fruition and for spells related to fertility, the goddess, the moon, and water magick.

Triangle

The triangle invokes trinities, from the Pagan Maiden, Mother, Crone to the Christian Father, Son, and Holy Spirit, as well as many others. It represents doorways, manifestation, culmination, and change. When finishing a project, stitch a small triangle in a corner or on the inside of a hem to ritually "close" the work and release the raised energy out into the universe to work your will. Triangle designs on oracle mats, tarot deck bags, and rune pouches align them with the energies needed to see into the past, present, and future. Use triangle designs for projects that need fire energy and for spells involving mental activities.

Square

Squares encompass the material world. Their sides relate to the four elements (earth, air, fire, and water) as well as the cardinal directions (north, east, south, and west). Frame embroidered designs in square frames to integrate the elements and directions into the finished spellwork. Altar cloths shaped as squares make positioning altar items easy. Use square designs for spells involving material things, prosperity, or the seasons. Square pieces of cloth can be used to make quick money and business-success spell pouches. Add a square patch pocket to any piece of clothing as a place to store coins or charms for bringing fortune into your life.

NUMBERS

Below are suggestions of how to incorporate number magick into your sewcraft. With each number after four, integrating number magick into a project becomes a little harder. Sewing with nine threads to invoke goddess energy into your project isn't very practical. Although, if you aren't working on something that has to be practical, go for it. You can include the energies of numbers five through nine by stitching the actual numerals in designs or repeating design elements a certain number of times. You can embroider stars with that number of points into hems or decorations. If you are hand sewing, keep track of the stitches and on the desired number say it and what energy you want. For example, for every eighth stitch, say, "And eight for good luck."

Look over the magickal energies of the numbers below to find which ones to use for various intentions.

Zero

It can be difficult to include zero's magickal energy of beginnings into sewing spellcraft. One must have something tangible to work with in order to sew. However, zero's shape, meaning, and energy correspond to the circle. You can use a circle to represent zero in projects if needed.

One

One represents the source and grounding. Use one thread for basting projects, visualizing the thread being the starting point for your project. Projects like circle pouches and pressing cloths embody one's energy, as they involve a single piece of fabric.

Two

Two is the number of balance, cooperation, and the Goddess and God. Most often counted cross stitch uses two strands of floss to make a cross out of two stitches. Use cross stitches on spellwork for invoking the Goddess and God, for healing emotions, or for restoring balance.

Three

Like the triangle, three invokes trinities. It is a number of action. When I am tying off my thread, I will knot it three times, saying, "spirit, mind, body," "Maiden, Mother, Crone," or another triple concept that aligns with my intent. Three ribbons are braided in witch cords. Use three strands of embroidery floss when working on a design for spellwork that needs a sense of immediacy or a boost of speed.

Four

Four shares the symbolism of the elements and directions with the square. It is the number of creativity. As an even number, it amplifies the balancing energies of the number two. Use four different colors that harmonize with each other in blankets, robes, and jewelry to bring equilibrium to yourself. Recruit the four elements into your spellworking by working four decorative borders around your embroidery designs or with flowers made from four cross stitches in a cross pattern.

Five

Five is a number of change, but this is change through struggle. It is the number of spirit, often symbolized in the pentagram. Use it in projects that involve marriage, health, and love.

Six

Six represents the sun, security, inner peace, and responsibility. Use it in projects that involve luck in gambling, divination, astral projection, and ESP.

Seven

Seven represents the moon, intuition, and wisdom. Use it in projects meant to increase focus, safety, or rest.

Eight

Eight represents messages and communication, as well as good luck. Use it in projects for abundance and power and in those that are meant to help with making decisions (such as oracle mats).

Nine

Nine represents the Goddess, change, growth, and completion. Use it in projects to boost magickal workings and intent.

A NOTE ON SIGILS

For a more personal project, you can try making your own sigil. A sigil is a symbol that represents an intention. Sigils lend themselves to magickal embroidery, as concentration on the design builds the magickal intention and power into the sigil itself. Release the power of the sigil by either putting it away where it can be forgotten or burning it. If you decide to embroider a sigil and burn it, make sure you use only 100 percent natural fibers.

MAGICKAL ALPHABETS FOR EMBROIDERY

There are many magickal alphabets you can use to charge various sewing projects. Runes, the Theban alphabet (also known as the witch's alphabet), and Enochian are all well suited to embroider designs. If you want to be discreet, they can be added the inside of a hem or a lining. Or you can turn them into border elements or even incorporate them into your embroidery designs.

Elder Futhark

Elder Futhark runes are one of the best-known magickal alphabets and date from the first century CE. Their purpose is a matter of debate, but some magickal or ritual uses are suggested in inscriptions found throughout Europe. They lend themselves to magickal crafts related to divination as well as those that invoke Norse deities and their powers.

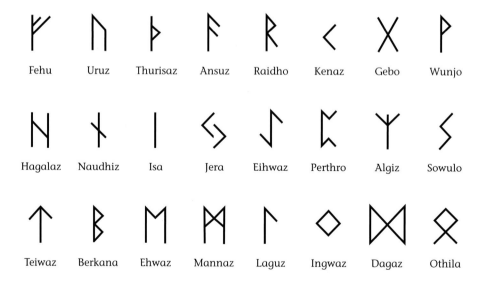

Ogham Alphabet

Ogham is an alphabet dating from before the fifth century CE. Surviving inscriptions are of names, indicating that it was originally used as marking land ownership. Within Pagan traditions, the Ogham has been adapted into a divinatory tool. It is well suited for craft projects involving divination and Celtic deities and their powers, for embroidering your craft name, and for quick cross stitch magick spells (as it involves only backstitching).

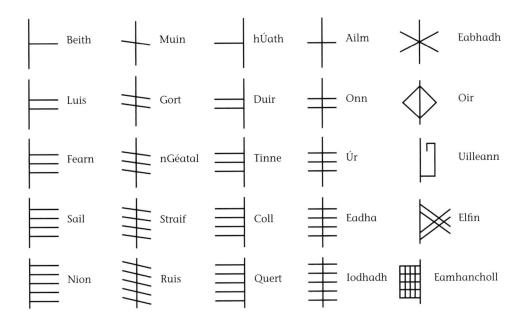

Theban Alphabet

The Theban alphabet is a sixteenth-century writing system. Adopted by Wicca, it has been used as a cipher for magickal workings, Books of Shadows, and spells for years. Due to its one-to-one correlation to the English alphabet, it can be useful in embroidered projects to enhance the magickal intentions or as a way to obscure your magickal workings if needed.

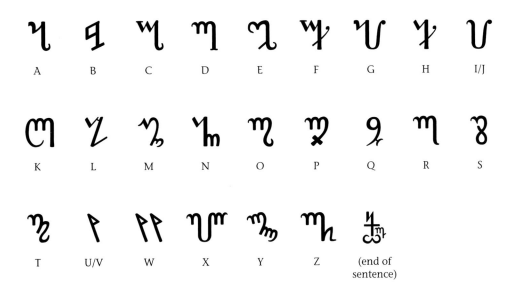

Enochian Alphabet

Another sixteenth-century alphabet, the Enochian, or Angelic, symbols were recorded by John Dee and Edward Kelley. The alphabet is used in Enochian magick. Like Theban, Enochian has English equivalents, so it can be used in embroidery samplers and spells. Due to its association with angels, it would be well suited to spellwork regarding the spirit.

A	B	C/Ch/K	D	E	F	G/J	H	I
L	M	N	O	P/Ph	Q/Qu	R	S	T
U/V	X	Y	Z					

Magickal Timing for Sewing

Timing your sewing spellcraft to moon phases or days of the week follows much of the same guidelines as for any other spellwork. The difference is that most sewing projects take longer than a single day. If you wish to work in alignment with certain days, you can work on that project only on those days. In this case, spend a little time breaking down the project by steps. Figure out how much time each step takes, and then schedule the project over the number of days it will take you to complete. For example, if you want to work on the Simple Square Altar Cloth on page 94 only on Thursday to tap into its inherent spiritual energy, schedule your project as follows:

> ***First Thursday of the Waxing Moon:*** Cut out fabric.
> ***Second Thursday of the Waxing Moon:*** Sew the main parts.
> ***Third Thursday of the Waxing Moon:*** Finish.

This schedule taps not only into the energies of Thursday but also into the waxing moon, and depending on how you schedule it, the finishing falls within the span of the full moon.

This way of sewing does extend the time it takes to finish a project. Planning it out ahead of time ensures the project gets finished, rather than ending up at the bottom of an "in progress" pile.

DAYS OF THE WEEK

Sunday

Sunday is the multipurpose day of the week. Aligned with the sun, success, personal power and growth, and healing, this day is good to work on any project. If you have a habit of starting projects but not finishing them, start on Sunday. Before you begin work, call on the sun to bless your work and to lend you the energy to see it through to the end.

Monday

Monday is the moon's day. It embodies the energies of emotion, intuition, dreams, and psychic abilities. Make dream pillows, kitchen and home linens, aprons, curtains, and spell bags on Monday.

Tuesday

Tuesday is a day of action. Justice, bravery, and strength are its energies. Sew work clothes, spell bags for courage and victory, and charms for social justice and triumph in legal matters.

Wednesday

Wednesday is a day of communication and wisdom energies. Make or start projects related to school clothes, book and school bags, journal covers, and even bookmarks to tap into the day's intelligence energies. If you are a crafter who sells their wares, Wednesday is a good day to make those items.

Thursday

Thursday is another good day for projects for overcoming legal issues. Make spell bags for prosperity and luck to tap into Thursday's abundance energy. Make, repair, or enchant work clothes.

Friday

Friday is a day aligned with love, both romantic and platonic. It is a day for spellwork related to happiness and beauty. Make bed linens to encourage more passion in your relationship. Create clothing and accessories, such as the Glamour Scarf on page 122, to enhance your own personal style. Friday is a good day for creating spell bags for healing, love, and beauty.

Saturday

Saturday is a day of closure. Finish projects on this day to release the magickal energy into the world. Make curtains, door mats and rugs, wreaths, and protective pouches on this day to tap into its protective energies. Work binding spells like those starting on page 79. As Saturday has cleansing energies, wash fabric for upcoming projects on this day.

MOON PHASES

To work with moon phases on projects, follow these guidelines:

New Moon

Plan projects during the new moon. Use a calendar with the moon phases marked out to decide when you will be sewing. Look through books, magazines, and blogs for ideas. Gather your supplies onto your altar and give them a new moon blessing to start your project off on a positive note.

Waxing Moon

Prepare fabric, pin patterns, and cut fabric during the waxing moon. Draw the building energy of the waxing moon into your project. When you sew, visualize the energy imbuing every stitch until it glows.

Full Moon

Sew, visualizing the energy imbuing every stitch until it glows. Add decorative elements to add power to your project.

Waning Moon

Sew, finish, and clean up during the waning moon. Use the releasing energy of the waning moon to send your magick out into the universe. If you are working on a project for banishing, warding, or returning, draw the shrinking energy of the waning moon into the materials.

SEASONAL SEWING

Structuring your sewing around the seasons is as good as any other organizational method out there. It has the added benefit of aligning your projects with the energies of the season as well as being traditional to some cultures.

Winter

Winter is a time of planning and sorting (if you haven't done so in autumn). In the Northern Hemisphere, the colder weather urges us to stay indoors. It's a time to rest and restore as the nights lengthen and daylight is in short supply. Read books, magazines, and blogs for ideas on projects to make in the new year. Take out your calendar and start plotting out what projects you'll be working on when, taking into account things like moon phases, sabbats, and other holidays. This is a time to stock up on fleece and other cold-weather fabrics that go on sale, as well as winter-themed prints. In the United States of America, January brings sales on linens and storage supplies. Pick up extra boxes and containers to pack away the material you bought on sale; make sure to properly label them so they don't get lost. Tackle your mending pile. Work on small, warm, and last-minute projects: socks, scarves, replacement mittens, and so on. Make the Protective Cowl on page 125. Get ready for spring by making fabric flowers for your altar as well as Imbolc and Ostara.

Spring

Spring brings new vitality to our lives. Sew aprons for gardening and foraging. Look ahead and make garlands for Beltane and Midsummer. Work on fertility spell bags, baby blankets, bibs, and clothes. Take a length of flowy, delicate silk, give it a narrow hem, and wear it on those days that still have a bit of chill in the air. Knit or crochet a lightweight throw. Look forward to the end of the year and start cutting out the pieces for a quilt. Make rugs to catch the mud that people and animals will track in. Set out bits of thread and yarn for birds to use in nests (or use them in magick like the Thread Snippets spell on page 71). If you didn't do a fall cleanup of your crafting area, now's the time for a spring-cleaning. Have supplies you know you won't use? Set up a swap with other crafting friends. Make it a fun outing, a time to reconnect after the long cold winter. Air out bedding and go over it to see what might need to be repaired and what needs to be scrapped. Spring is for beginnings. Ideas that have hibernated all winter long are ready to be realized. Pack away winter's things; make linen sachets filled with dried lavender, rosemary, and thyme to tuck in with them to keep them fresh and safe. In the United States of America, March is National Crafting Month and National Quilting Month, which can mean sales at various hobby and craft stores.

Summer

Summer sees people out and about, leaving the indoors behind. That doesn't mean they aren't also crafting. Sew a picnic blanket for Midsummer. Work on prosperity spell pouches to store the abundance of summer. Make skirts and shorts to take advantage of the warmer weather. Make floppy hats to protect your scalp from sunburn. If you have young children, go through their clothes, turning pants into shorts so they can be worn just a little while longer. Engage children in crafting by making capes, no-sew tutus, masks, and other costumes together. Invite friends over for tea (or wine) and crafting parties. Piece together the quilt you started in the spring, sewing the warmth of summer into each stitch. Take your embroidery out with you and spend an hour sewing on your balcony, in your backyard, or at the park. Make cloth shopping bags to use at the farmers markets that run throughout the season, or make the Foraging Bag on page 165 for trips into nature for natural magick supplies. August sees another sale on linens and storage supplies, so if you can, stock up on ready-made items to charm and boxes in which to store them. Work on napkins and a tablecloth for Lughnasadh and Mabon feasts.

Fall

Fall is a time of finishing. Any projects that have been neglected should be completed. Time to pull out the heavy, cold-weather fabrics for scarves, blankets, and mittens. Go through your fabric and craft stashes for anything you know you won't use. Donate or trade them to clear out space. Hit up the craft and fabric stores after holidays to pick up fall-themed supplies for the next year. Now is the time for divination-related projects. Make the Tea-Stained Tarot Cloth on page 185 or the Tarot Sleeve on page 169. September is National Sewing Month in the United States, which brings more sales at craft and hobby stores. Halloween often serves up lots of supplies that can be used for Samhain celebrations. Use winter-themed fabric picked up the previous year to make Yule decorations and projects. Organize your crafting supplies and reading materials. Make sure that everything is where it should be, and replace any tools or items that have broken or gone missing. This way the long dark of winter can be spent planning instead of looking for that fat quarter of fabric or pattern or skein of yarn. Finish the quilt you have been working on all year long, so you have something warm to snuggle under as the air cools. Go over your sewing journal to review the projects you worked on over the year. Make notes of what was accomplished, what magick you made, the results, and so on. This will be an important tool come winter when you start planning your next year of magickal sewing.

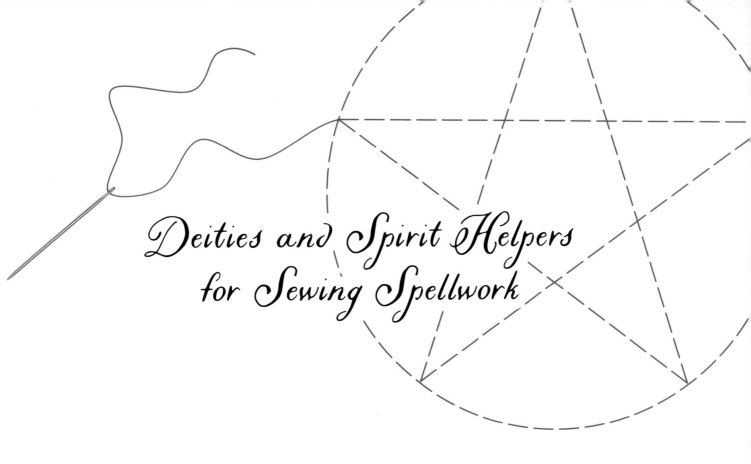

Deities and Spirit Helpers for Sewing Spellwork

*N*early all religions have deities associated with sewing or crafting arts. You can find a list of various gods and goddesses on page 215. There are many ways you can work with a deity in your sewing spellwork. You can invoke them as you sew, asking them to add their energies to the task. Call on Lugh, the Celtic god of weaving, if you are starting a weaving or knitting project to bless it. Tools and materials can be dedicated to them. For example, a length of linen can be dedicated to Hulda, a Germanic goddess of flax cultivation, before use. Or dedicate your scissors to Hephaestus, the Greek god of crafters. Place representations of Minerva (the Roman goddess of crafts and magick), Ananse (the West African spider god), or Uttu (the Mesopotamian goddess of weaving) on your altar.

When working with deities, be culturally sensitive. Some deities are specific to a religion—Sarasvati, the Hindu goddess of arts, for example. Before you decide to work with a god or goddess outside of your particular path or culture, research them, the religion they belong to, and the culture they come from. Some Pagans will treat deities like archetypes that can be plugged into a ritual, choosing ones from around the world for their "exotic" appeal. This is due in part to the influence of ancient Greek and Roman cultures that would assimilate the deities of conquered cultures. Rather than perpetuating that colonialist act, show the deities you are looking to work with respect and learn what you can about them. Go so far as to meditate and journey to meet with them and ask if you can work with them. Respect and humility will go a long way toward ensuring a healthy relationship.

There are just as many spirit helpers that can be called on to aid you in your sewing spellwork as deities. Spirit helpers include any faeries, genius loci, folk heroes, or astral creatures. They can be invited to help with projects, to guard workspaces, and to add their energies to spells. In many ways they are as helpful as deities to work with. Spirit helpers tend to be more personal, I've found. They perform a role that is less an advisor and mentor and more of a partner.

Of these two kinds of magickal help, I work with Arachne and suffer house gnomes who will often hide my tools. Both provide an extra dimension to my spellwork, keeping the thread between the magick and the mundane, even when I am cursing over a crooked seam.

WORKSHOP PROTECTORS

Whether they are called Nisse, Tomte, or hobgoblins, the household spirits that protect the home and help with the chores share a few common features. They nearly all require payment for their work, usually in the form of food and respect. They are known to cause mischief, ranging from small pranks (missing items, pratfalls) to actual harm (dragging people out of bed, tossing people over roofs) for those who slack in their work or tease the spirits.

Having a workshop protector, a house spirit who has taken up residence in your home and who watches over your sewing space and implements, can add an extra dimension to your magickal workings. A workshop protector can serve as a constant guard of your work, keeping ill-meaning faeries and those who would use your fabric scissors on paper at bay. It can be a great way to tap into the local magickal energies of the place through this genius loci. You may even be able to extend your working relationship with the hob to other faery folk in the area.

It's up to you whether the presence of a household spirit would be welcome. Having a workshop protector might be a comforting presence. Or the maintenance and possibility of missing items (or worse!) might not appeal to you. They can be mischievous, as Penny Parker points out in *Farmhouse Witchcraft*: "I have found that they [faeries] get into my sewing things and play war with my pins and needles (they make swords) as I find them on the floor and other odd places."

Attracting a House Spirit

If you decide you want to try to attract a hob, first make your workspace as attractive as possible. This is not meant merely in the sense of appearance. It should be a place where one would like to spend time. It might seem against reason that you have to maintain a space to attract a spirit to help maintain it, but house spirits are drawn to spaces where there is already a careful and caring energy.

Many house spirits require their own room, with a bed, table, and chair. You can set up a "faery room" with miniature furniture in an out-of-the-way place, like a shelf or cupboard, or install a faery door in a wall for the hob to use. You can also make one of the House Gnomes on page 113 as a stand-in and enticement for the spirit, as some have been known to inhabit a small doll or statue.

Take time to sit quietly in your workspace. Ground yourself and meditate, focusing on sending out welcoming energies. Ask if there is a house spirit and if they want to make contact with you. Invite them to stay and join you in your creative endeavors. If a house spirit has chosen to move in, they will make their presence known to you.

If a house spirit takes up residence, make sure to offer them payment for their assistance. Traditionally, this involves setting out food: porridge with butter or cakes and ale or milk. You can leave a small portion out before you go to bed. The hob will take what they want, and the rest you can dispose of the next day. Many house spirits, faeries, and gods take only the essence of the food, and so if you find yourself in a situation where leaving out food is a problem (because of pets, pests, or scarcity), you can substitute the food with crafted offerings: salt-dough models or the like. Put the facsimiles out with the same intention and ritual as you would the food.

Sometimes the spirits we attract or those we inherit when we move into our homes don't mesh with the household. The first, best step is to try to find out what is setting the spirit off. Meditation with the intention of making contact and talking things out is your first step. However, if you have tried to make peace with a pesky pixie and yet they still insist on blunting your scissors and tangling your yarn, it might be time to serve an eviction notice.

Try first asking the spirit nicely to leave. It's always a good idea to try politeness first, especially with a spirit that can get physical if offended. Thank them for their presence, protection, and service and then ask them to leave. If that doesn't work, try this time-honored solution from fairy tales and folklore: send them packing by providing them with a new suit of clothes. Sew a miniature dress or pants and shirt from fine cloth (linen is the traditional choice). Leave it out where the house spirit can find it. Delighted with the new duds, they will leave, never to return.

If bribery doesn't work, you will have to try banishment. Iron, garlic, salt, black pepper, sandalwood, mistletoe, cinnamon, clove, and bay are said to repel faeries. Make a pouch filled with herbs and a nail and hang it over your space to drive the house spirit away.

Spells and

Magick

The Witch's Tools

When we think of magick in a Wiccan or Pagan context, the image of the ceremonial ritual, the quarters called, the candles lit, and the words spoken comes to mind. With cottage or hedge magick we see the witch standing over the stove, her saucepan, or her cauldron, stirring in herbs and saying words to effect change. It is an image that has enough similarities to ritual, "circle" magick, that we can easily accept it. (That kitchen witchery has a longer, more established practice helps, too.)

It isn't as easy to make the same correspondences to craft magick. Often the goal of creating an item is in the final object itself. The process of the construction is granted none of the care that ritual is. Oh, attention might be paid to the components, and the final object may be charged once it is finished. But what of the steps in between? The actual sewing, snipping of threads, cutting the fabric? What regard is given to those acts? What care is taken in treating our scissors and pins, our tape measures and marking chalk as the tools of change they are?

THE SEWING MACHINE AS CAULDRON

A sewing machine looks as much unlike a cauldron as you can get. Even the earliest hand-crank Singers have too many moving parts, too many man-made energies to match the simplicity of the pot, open to the ingredients of magick. It takes a flexibility of thinking, an expansive imagination, to look beyond the physical differences and see the similarities they share.

Each is a tool of change. Each allows the witch to create magick. Each can provide a focus for Will and intent.

What I propose is a shift in thinking to embrace the act of magickal creation in all its parts. Viewing the whole process from start to finish can deepen your connection to the intended use of your craft. It connects you to the work in a way that, like meditation, keeps you in the moment. And by infusing your process with ritual, you can find new ways of engaging with your path.

THE SEWING BASKET AS ALTAR

For those without a dedicated sewing space, there are still ways to have a magick space in which to work. Simplest is to co-opt your sewing basket to serve double duty as a mobile altar. Sewing baskets are ideal for this task. They can contain everything you need for both magickal and mundane means. If you aren't out of the broom closet, so to speak, no one will guess that the basket has anything to do with magick. It's portable, and there are so many varieties available you are sure to find one that suits your purpose and personality perfectly.

To use your sewing basket as an altar, organize it as you would a standard altar. Set one side or end as "north" and use organizer dividers to keep your tools in the quarters they belong to. Alternatively, make an altar cloth you can pull out either to drape on the basket or to set up your temporary altar as you work.

Whichever way you decide on, make sure to keep your basket organized and well stocked. Rummaging through a tangle of bias tape, thread, buttons, and lace sets a chaotic note in your ritual work. Make setup and cleanup part of your ritual. It makes for effective bookends to your work and is practical.

MAKING YOUR OWN SEWING
BOOK OF SHADOWS

A sewing Book of Shadows is a record of your sewing spellcraft, allowing you to look back at what you have done. You can see what has worked and what hasn't and adjust your witchcraft accordingly. It can be as fancy or as simple as you wish. My own spans several lined journals, bristling with tabs and stuffed with fabric swatches, coupons for JoAnn Fabric and Craft Stores, and random scraps of paper. Take a moment to browse your local office supply store to find a notepad, journal, or binder that suits your purposes (and pick up some binder clips to use in your sewing).

Keeping records, even if only for yourself, makes good sense. In the future you won't be left wondering if you used cinnamon or cloves in your healing pouch or if you sewed your cloak during the waxing or full moon. It's all there.

If you make it a habit to look over past projects once or twice a year, you can glean insights into your personal sewing spellwork. Patterns will emerge. Were there certain fabrics that worked better for you? Were there types of projects you continuously failed to finish? Perhaps you see that you have had more success with projects related to your

Sewing Book of Shadows Sample Page

PROJECT:

DATE:

● ◑ ○ ◐

GOAL:

_____
_____
_____
_____
_____
_____
_____

DEITY INVOKED:

_____
_____

CORRESPONDENCES:

_____
_____
_____
_____
_____
_____

MATERIALS:

_____
_____
_____
_____
_____
_____
_____

FABRIC SAMPLES

NOTES

own success more than those made for others. The answers to these questions can be used to plan out future projects.

A sample project journal page is offered on the previous page. Feel free to use it as is or modify it to your tastes.

Keep a page at the front of your Book of Shadows with a list of projects you want to make. You can then schedule them according to any magickal timing you wish (seasonally, astrologically, by moon phase, etc.). You can work out how long a project will take, make a list of what materials you'll need, and write notes on what herbs, crystals, and so on you want to include or what deities you wish to invoke as you work. If you engage in any divination before you start a project, you can note those results on the project page as well. Jot down notes before, during, and after the project. Write whatever is important to you.

Swatches can be attached with glue or double-sided tape. I like to give my swatches a trim with pinking shears. This keeps the fabric from fraying and I like the way it looks. Make a note of where you got the swatch from, in case you need to get more later. Also, noting any washing instructions from the bolt will save you grief later on when you are trying to remember if you should be using hot or cold water, using high or low heat, or line drying the fabric.

PREPARING YOUR TOOLS

Before starting a project, especially one that is magickal in nature, you want to prepare your tools and materials. This involves more than just gathering everything together in one place. You'll want to take some time to cleanse and charge items. You might even want to mark some of your tools with sigils related to the purpose of your project. Aligning the energies of your tools and materials to a specific purpose helps focus your intent, making the end product even more powerful.

Cleansing

In many ways, cleansing your sewing tools is much like cleansing any other magickal implements. Your goal is to clear any preexisting energies on the item so that you can charge it with a new purpose. Many of the usual ways of cleansing, however, aren't well suited for sewing aids. A water bath will ruin your sewing machine or rust your scissors. Fire is a no go for fabric and thread. This is where you have to be flexible, using the method best suited for the item, rather than a one-size-cleanses-all procedure.

Sun or moon bathing is effective if you have a window that lets in adequate light. Moon bathing is best when it can happen over an entire cycle, full moon to full moon, so you may have to plan accordingly.

More simply, and faster besides, is to smoke cleanse the items with sage. The scent might cling to fabric, however, and so take that into consideration if you are making something for a person with scent sensitivities. If you need to launder fabric before it is used, you can incorporate cleansing into that process. See Laundering Fabric and Clothes on page 75 for more details.

Charging

Once you have cleansed your items, you want to charge them with energies aligned to the purpose of your project. You want to keep this simple and specific. Think about what this project is for and what you intend for the end result. If you are making a scarf for a friend you want to cheer up, focus on the friendship and joy aspects of the project. If you are making an altar cloth, focus on the sacred aspect.

As with cleansing, there are many ways to charge items, some better suited to sewing implements and materials than others.

You can charge your tools and materials with your own energies. Hold the tools in your hands, or hold your hands over them, palms facing the tools. Take several deep, cleansing breaths and envision the project you will make. Think of all the aspects of this project: its purpose, the energies it will encompass, even the moods and feelings it should invoke. You should also summon your excitement for this project, as that will be a powerful catalyst for visualization and act as a magnifier for your charging efforts. If it is a magick item, see the results of its workings. Imagine all of these, filling your body with your intentions until you feel as if you are bursting with the energy. Then pour that energy out of your hands into the tools.

If you are working on a project that you won't be personally using or one that you don't want tied so intimately to your own being, use crystals or herbs to charge your tools. For both methods, time the charging to coincide with the phases of the moon. Charge an object over several nights of a waxing moon for projects that are meant to attract, meant to increase, or for gain. For projects meant to banish, protect, or repel, charge the tools and materials over several nights of the waning moon.

For crystal charging, place the crystal near or on the tools and materials you wish to charge. Envision the vibrations from the crystal entering the tools, filling them with the energies you need for the project. You can leave the crystals to charge up to three days. Keep the crystals near you as you work to provide continued support.

Herbal charging is similar to the above. Lay sachets of your chosen herbs on fabrics or tools. You can even bury them in the loose, dried herbs, if you have enough. Loose herbs should only be used with fabric or tools without moving parts, to avoid the risk of jamming the works. This method is particularly useful with fabrics, especially if the herb has a pleasant scent, such as lavender or rose petals. Make sure to shake out any herbs that might cling to the fabric before using it.

You can also charge projects once you have finished them. This signals that the item is ready for use and allows you to set it to its ultimate purpose. For example, when making the Prosperity Sachets on page 204, you would charge your materials and tools before starting the sachets, and after they are completed, you would charge them as a final "seal" on the magick.

Sewcraft

his is where the theoretical rubber meets the practical road in sewing magick. The following pages cover rituals and spells that can be used in all the steps involved in making the projects in the second half of the book. From winding the bobbin at the start of your project to pressing the final seam, these practices weave magickal intention and thinking into your work. As with every other aspect of spellcraft, repetition and habit will strengthen your workings. By practicing the rituals whenever you engage in sewing magick, you will find that they not only become second nature but also cause a shift in how you approach and engage in even your mundane sewing.

Also included are spells that take the most ordinary of sewing supplies and use them for powerful folk magick. Buttons and thread are versatile components to magick—you just need to use your imagination. I highly recommend using items that have a connection to you or the spell you'll be working. I keep a small box in which I store buttons from clothing my children have outgrown (and that have been worn to tatters) should I ever need to work magick for them. Use scraps of fabric from shirts you've loved when sewing spells for yourself so that the magick will be immediately tied to you. You can use the color correspondences chart on page 219 to choose a thread color aligned to your purpose.

WITCH BOTTLE

If you sew a lot, you end up with used sewing machine needles. You don't want to just toss those needles into the garbage. They could poke through the bag or fall

out and injure someone. The standard suggestion for needle disposal is to either wrap the needles in duct tape to cover the sharp ends or to place them in a container like a prescription bottle and dispose of that.

I'd rather put those sharp pointy ends to a magickal use than throw them out. So, inspired by the witch bottle in Cunningham and Harrington's book *The Magical Household*, I started my own variation.

Witch bottles are a form of decoy magick. They are meant to provide a diversion to and give protection from evil intentions.

Start with a bottle with a lid: a prescription bottle, a spice jar, or a baby food jar are all acceptable receptacles. The lid should be a screw top. Using an awl or a drill fitted with a narrow bit, punch a hole in the lid.

Keep the bottle, with the lid on, near your sewing machine. When you are ready to dispose of a needle, take a moment. Hold the needle in your hand, and center and ground. Visualize a line of needles and pins surrounding your home. They jut out like spears. Their points shine with deadly purpose. Anything that means you harm—any negative thoughts, jealousy, unfriendly entities, or harmful energy—is pierced by these needles. It sticks fast and cannot make it into your home. Feel the determined, protective energy of all these needles and pins. Nothing can get past them to harm you.

As you visualize this, place the needle into the bottle. Reaffirm that all the sharps in it are there to protect you. Thank them again for this new task they perform for you. Put the bottle back. Then move on to the next project without worry or concern, letting the needle do its job.

Once the bottle is full, add sea salt and a protective herb like rosemary. Cover the hole with a bit of masking tape and mark it with a protective sign. You can bury it near the entrance to your home or stash it somewhere near your workspace where it won't be disturbed.

THREAD SNIPPETS

Thread has been used for millennia in witchcraft. It makes an appearance in folklore and religious rites, such as its use by the three Fates in Greek mythology. You can tap into this simple but potent magick with the following wish spell.

In the spring, hang an empty suet feeder outside. As you accumulate snippets of thread while you sew, name them for your wishes. Place the thread into the suet feeder. As the birds take the thread away to use in their nests, your wishes will go out into the world to manifest. When spring ends, fill the suet feeder with food as a gift of thanks for the birds' help.

Avian Divination

Ornithomancy is the practice of divination through observation of the movement of birds. By combining this ancient augury with the thread snippet spell, you can look for omens based on your wishes. After placing your thread snippets in the suet feeder, observe what kind of birds come for the nest-building material. Consult a guide to magickal symbolism to see what the visiting bird could mean. If, for example, a sparrow visits the feeder, you can interpret that as a sign your wishes will have a good chance of coming true, as sparrows are seen as symbols of peace and joy.

WITCH STITCHES

You don't have to make something from scratch to imbue it with magick. Add some witch stitches to anything ready made to mark it and imbue it with the energies you need. Start by picking a thread color to suit your purpose. For instance, if you are going to a job interview, use a green thread. If you want to charm your child's backpack to help protect them on their walks to and from school, use a pink thread.

Turn the article of clothing or the item you want to charm inside out and find a seam, inside hem, or other place that isn't visible from the outside. Stitch three small cross stitches. As you work, envision the outcome you want. Say,

By these stitches three,
My will be done; so mote it be.

Knot the thread and turn the article right-side out again.

If you ever need to add a new magickal energy to the clothes, remove the witch stitches before laundering and then work new stitches.

SPOOLING YOUR MAGICK

Thread literally binds a project together. You can harness that power before you even begin to sew by charging the spool of thread with your intent. This can be as simple as holding the spool in your hands and breathing your intention into it.

For bigger projects or more complicated projects, you can anchor that intention by marking the spool. Choose runes, sigils, power words, or personal power symbols that correspond with your purpose. Perhaps you are sewing a purse on which you will set a prosperity spell. In this case you can simply write dollar signs on the label or around the rim of the top of the spool. As you sew, the spool spins, empowering the thread. It also serves as a reminder of your purpose, keeping you focused on your intent as you sew.

If the project you are working on has to do with banishing or binding, write the symbols on the bottom of the spool. For instance, if you are working on a blanket for a friend who is ill, draw the rune Isa to break up the disease that is plaguing them. You can use any symbol that represents what you are trying to banish. Even a frowning face will do, as long as it has meaning for you.

Use this spell when winding your bobbin thread, marking the spool it will come from before winding, for added oomph. When you are sewing, visualize your intention being linked together, as above so below. For those sewists with advanced visualization skills, a bobbin holding thread charged with one intent can be used with a spool charged with another to create nuanced spellwork.

Bobbin threads are best suited for spells that affect interior, secret, or hidden spaces, while thread from spools is best suited for spells that affect exterior, visible, or open spaces. With this in mind, an example of a multithread spell would be a scarf that has bobbin threads charmed to protect the wearer from a sore throat, while the spool thread has been charmed to protect the wearer from the germs of others. An interior and exterior magickal defense, along with proper nutrition and exercise, can go a long way toward keeping the sewist healthy during cold and flu season.

Charming your thread this way will mean that it might not be usable for other projects. A spool charmed for prosperity won't be appropriate for a binding spell, for example. The more specific the charmed purpose, the more limited the spool will be. You can charm your thread for more general purposes, however, to use in multiple projects. Otherwise, make sure you have the right amount of thread for your specific project. Leftover thread could be used as witch stitches to reinforce the spell or saved for any future repairs.

PRAYER STRIPS

Across religions and worldwide there is a tradition of tying strips of fabric to trees as prayer or wishes. In some areas strips of linen from the bed of a sick person were tied to the trees. As the strip broke down, the illness was said to leave the patient.

In my yard grows a golden curly willow I planted years ago. Grandmother Willow has been the recipient of many prayer strips over the years. It is comforting to look out the window and see them waving in the wind. Even better is to one day notice that a strip is gone, having completely disintegrated and released my prayer.

You can tie your own prayer or wish to a tree. This can be as simple as tying a thread to a tree branch. Or you can write a prayer upon a strip of muslin, or even embroider it. Make sure the fabric you use is natural. Amplify your intentions by choosing thread or fabric in a color suited to your prayer. You can even dress the prayer strip with oils that match the energies you wish to send out.

If you have a tree you've already established a connection with, you can tie your prayer to it. Otherwise, look for a tree that speaks to you. When you have found one, talk to it, asking if it will carry your prayer for you. If the answer is yes, then proceed. If no, respect the tree's decision and move on.

When you attach your prayer strip to a tree, drape it over a branch rather than tying it. Make an offering of thanks in the form of water or another gift to the tree. Don't look back once you have made your prayer. As the cloth waves in the wind and falls apart, your prayer or wish is carried out into the universe.

Some trees are better suited for certain prayers than others. If you don't have a tree you already work with, you can look for one that matches your need:

Healing: Apple, elder, lemon, lime, oak, walnut, or willow

Love: Apple, apricot, hawthorn, maple, orange, or peach

Prosperity: Apple, cedar, elder, or pine

Protection: Ash, aspen, birch, cypress, elder, elm, hawthorn, hazel, juniper, linden, rowan, walnut, or willow

Laundering Fabric and Clothes

Clothes are one of our first lines of defense, both magickal and practical. We wear coats, scarves, and gloves to protect us from the elements. When we need a boost of confidence, we wear our favorite outfit. Our clothing can be invested in glamour magick. Some of us might even have special garments for working spells or ritual. As versatile and important as our clothes are, it makes sense to see how we can add magick to every aspect of them, including our laundry routine. Laura Tempest Zakroff covers this idea in *The Witch's Cauldron*: "Clothes are another layer of protection and, as many fashion designers know, are a type of physically transforming glamour. Imagine any of the herbal baths we just covered bringing those same energies to the clothes you are wearing. It really kicks the magick up another level, because it's another reminder of your intention."

Magickal laundering isn't limited to our clothing. It can also be used as a way to imbue fabric with magickal energies before you start the work. Perhaps you are working on an article of clothing, something you'll wear to a function where you want to impress. When preshrinking your fabric, you could add an herbal infusion—perhaps made from cinnamon and ginger—to the rinse cycle to add an energy of success to the fabric.

Or maybe you'll be making a scarf for a friend to keep them warm and healthy throughout the winter months. You can run the finished scarf through the air dry cycle of your dryer along with several wool dryer balls anointed with eucalyptus essential oils. This adds healing vibrations to the fabric.

There's been a surge in interest in natural and homemade laundry products over the last few years. Whether for ecological or economic reasons, people want fewer chemicals and more control over their laundry soap. This is a boon to the witch, as a quick Pinterest search will reveal hundreds of different recipes they can use and modify for magickal purposes. Rather than cover that whole field and get bogged down in the great Borax debate, I'm going to focus on some specific ways to turn a household chore into an essential practice of your sewing spellcraft: laundry rinses.

LAUNDRY RINSES

Laundry rinses require only two ingredients: distilled white vinegar and essential oils. You will use it the same way you would use fabric softener: either add it during the rinse cycle or to the fabric softener dispenser. Start with pouring 2 ounces of distilled white vinegar into a small jar with a tight-fitting lid. Add 12 to 15 drops of your chosen essential oil. Shake to mix.

Suggested essential oils:

Healing: Eucalyptus, lotus, myrrh, rosemary

Hex Breaking: Bergamot, myrrh, rosemary

Love: Clove, jasmine, rose

Luck: Cinnamon

Money: Bergamot, mint, pine

Peace: Gardenia, hyacinth, rose

Protection: Myrrh, rosemary

Purification: Cinnamon, clove, lavender

You aren't limited to only essential oils, either. The same laundry rinse can be made by infusing the vinegar with herbs. Place fresh or dried herbs into the jar and pour the vinegar over them. Place the lid on, give it a good shake, and let it sit for at least 24 hours in a dark place. Afterward, strain out the herbs and your laundry rinse is ready.

Suggested herbs to use in your wash preparation:

Exorcism: Clove, clover, mint, rosemary, sagebrush

Happiness: Catnip, lavender

Healing: Cinnamon, lemon balm, mint, nettle, peppermint, plantain, rosemary, thistle, thyme

Love: Basil, catnip, chamomile, chickweed, cinnamon, clove, clover, ginger, lavender, peppermint, rosemary, thyme

Luck: Nutmeg, rose

Peace: Lavender

Protection: Basil, cinnamon, clove, lavender, marigold, mint, plantain, sage

Purification: Lavender, peppermint, rosemary, sagebrush, thyme

Success: Cinnamon, clover, ginger, lemon balm

Wealth: Chamomile, cinnamon, clove, clover, ginger, goldenrod, mint, nutmeg

Before use, hold the jar and charge the rinse with your intention. Visualize your outcome and push that energy into the rinse. Add the rinse to your washer and then walk away. Let the magick work its way into the fibers of your clothes.

DRYER BALLS

Dryer balls are felted wool balls used as an alternative to dryer sheets. They bounce around the dryer with the clothes, "beating" them to soften the fabric. They also cut drying times by absorbing moisture. You can buy them or make your own.

To use them for magickal purposes, add 2 to 3 drops of an appropriate essential oil to the dryer balls and pop them into the dryer with your fabric or clothing. Visualize the energies of the essential oils being transferred to the fabric, imbuing it with the properties you want.

Magickal laundering isn't limited only to your current wardrobe, either. Pat Robertson once answered a question about thrift shop clothes needing to be exorcised, and while I disagree that a secondhand sweater might harbor demons, I do believe all clothes—new and used—should be laundered before they are worn. Khi Armand, in his book *Clearing Spaces*, suggests smoke cleansing any secondhand items you obtain, including clothes, to clear them of any energies from previous owners. To this end, use rosemary or lavender essential oils to remove any clinging energies. As you do so, envision the oils breaking up and dissipating any previous energies, leaving behind the clothes as a blank slate ready for you to wear.

LAVENDER LINEN SPRAY RECIPE

Linen sprays can be used to bolster magickal intent. Use the spray below in your nighttime routine to add a boost to the Dream Pillow on page 155. Before climbing into bed, spritz your blankets and pillow with a lavender linen spray to help lull you to the land of Nod. To make the linen spray, you need these:

2 ounces distilled water
2 teaspoons witch hazel
20 drops lavender essential oil

Pour the water into a spray bottle. Mix the witch hazel and lavender essential oil together. Add the witch hazel-lavender oil mix to the spray bottle. Shake well before each use.

PRESSING MAGICK

Of all the tools available to the sewist, the iron is the most perfectly balanced. It draws from all four elements, allowing the witchy sewist to bring whatever energy they need to a project. The metal of the soleplate represents earth. The heat represents fire. The water represents—you guessed it—water. And the steam represents air.

When ironing out your fabric before a project or pressing seams during construction, make use of the heat and steam from your iron to endow the material with your intentions. For example, if you are making an item for a friend, repeat the chant below while you work with the iron.

> *With fire and air, I press into thee*
> *Attributes of beauty and friendship; so mote it be.*

You can imbue the magickal properties of herbal infusions in your projects using your iron. There are two ways to go about it. Note: whichever method you choose, test it out beforehand on a swatch of the fabric you are working with to ensure that it won't stain or otherwise ruin the fabric.

Press Spray

Mix 1 part witch hazel with 3 parts distilled water and 10 drops of an essential oil aligned with your magickal intentions (see page 76 for suggestions) into a spray bottle. Spray onto fabric before pressing with the iron.

Herbal Infusion

Make an infusion of herbs aligned with your magickal intentions (see page 76 for full instructions and herb suggestions). Fill the water reservoir of your iron with this infusion and press the project as usual.

DISTILLED WATER

Distilled water is water with impurities removed. It is used for herbal infusions and decoctions and is especially suited for use in magickal sewing purposes.

Rainwater can be used in place of distilled water as it has a low mineral content. If you can't collect rainwater, however, you can distill tap water. The process requires a pot with a lid, a glass bowl, and a steamer tray.

Fill the pot with water and place the steamer tray with the glass bowl on the inside of the pot. The water in the pot should not reach over the edge of the glass bowl. Place the lid upside down on the pot. Heat the pot over medium heat. As the water heats up, it will turn into steam and rise to the lid, where it will condense back to water. This water will then drip down into the glass bowl. You can speed the process along by placing ice cubes on top of the lid.

When the desired amount of water has accumulated in the bowl, turn off the heat and pour the water into a glass container for storage. Use the distilled water for herbal infusions, in your steam iron, or for ritual.

Collecting rainwater or distilling water to be used in projects can be timed with the waxing moon. If your magickal intent is a project of banishing, do this work during the waning moon.

Binding Spells

inding spells are magick done to restrain a person's actions. This is often undertaken when someone is harming you through actions, through words, or magickally. The spells below are best done during the full moon. In the spoken parts of the spells insert the name of the person you are binding where "[name]" is written.

Many magick traditions have interdicts against hexing or offensive magick. Binding spells, however, are often acceptable as defensive magick. Traditionally, binding magick has been used on people who are causing harm. In today's reality, however, harm can come from other sources: companies that dump pollution into waterways, governments that oppress people, and even mental health disorders.

Consider the binding spell as a useful tool in activism as well as personal defense. If you suffer from ill health, whether mental or physical, performing a binding spell can enhance other healing work. It is in no way a substitution for professional help.

BINDING SCROLL

This spell is useful for when you need a temporary binding. You will be using red flannel, a popular fabric for working magick, as well as thread and pins. This spell also draws on the power of repetition and the number three.

Get a rectangular piece of red flannel. With three strands of black thread, embroider the name of the person you wish to bind. Straight stitches or backstitching work well. As you work, say,

One, two, three, I bind you, [name], from doing harm to yourself or to others.

Once you are done with the embroidery, roll or fold the flannel up, embroidery facing in. Using three more strands of black thread, sew around the edges of the flannel and tie a knot, binding it, saying,

Three by three, I bind you, [name], from doing harm to yourself or to others.

Finally, take three pins and pierce the flannel with them. Say,

Three by three by three, I bind you, [name], from doing harm to yourself or to others.

Place the flannel somewhere safe. When the time comes to undo the binding, remove the pins while saying,

Three by three by three, [name], you are free.

Cut away the thread wrapped around the flannel, saying,

Three by three, [name], you are free.

Unroll the flannel and remove the embroidery stitches. Say,

One, two, three, [name], you are free.

Bury or burn the flannel and thread. The pins can be reused after a cleansing.

POPPET SHROUD

If you have made the Sewing Poppet on page 108, you can use it in performing this binding spell. The poppet will stand in for the person (or corporation, idea, etc.) that is the target of the spell. For this spell, you'll need a poppet and also a rectangle of black muslin big enough to wrap around the poppet and act as a shroud.

Anoint the poppet and announce who it represents for the purpose of the spell. You can even write the name of the person on a piece of paper and pin it to the poppet. Lay the muslin out and place the poppet at its center. Pull the sides up and sew them together with the black thread so that the poppet is enclosed in the fabric. As you sew, say,

Stitch by stitch, you are bound, [name], from doing harm, either to others or yourself.

When the ritual is done, remove the shroud by loosening some of the stitches and sliding the poppet out. Bury the shroud, either in a place outdoors or even in a pot of soil if you don't have access to an outdoor spot. Cleanse your sewing poppet before you use it for anything else.

INTERFACING BINDING SPELL FOR HEALTH ISSUES

If you suffer from ill health, whether mental or physical, performing this binding spell can enhance other healing work done by medical professionals. However, it is in no way a substitution for professional help. In the spoken part of the spell, insert the name of the issue you are binding where "[issue]" is written. For example, if you are binding your anxiety, say, "I bind you, anxiety, from doing harm."

Cut a 4" × 4" square of black cloth. Using a fabric pen or pencil, mark a symbol representing the issue you are targeting with this spell. This can be as simple or as elaborate as you wish. To expand on the example above, you could write the rune Ingwaz with the circle slash symbol over it to represent your anxiety.

Cut a 3" piece of fusible webbing or hem tape. With the symbol facing in, fold the fabric in half, sandwiching the fusible webbing inside. Iron the fabric to fuse it together while saying,

By earth and air and fire and water,
I bind you, [issue], from doing me harm.

Place the fabric on your altar or in a spell bag. You may even want to carry it with you as a reminder that your issue is now bound.

MAGICKAL CRAFTIVISM

Over the last few years there has been a movement in the arts and crafts community to address political and social issues. This craftivism, a term coined by Betsy Greer, can be similarly used in spellcraft. While traditionally binding magick has been used on people, harm can come from other sources: companies that dump pollution into waterways, governments that oppress people, organizations that exploit workers, and so on. This concept has been embraced by the magickal community, and binding spells have been used in political contexts, most notably the movement in 2017 to work mass bindings against the United States president Donald Trump. The binding spells here can be easily adapted to marry your sewing spellcraft with your political and social passions.

BANISHING ILLNESS

An old bit of curative folk magick involves tying a piece of string around an inflicted body part. The string is then removed, without untying the knot, and thrown into a body of water or buried. This spell works off that concept and is useful for when tying a string wouldn't be possible or practical. You will need a piece of fabric, thread, needle (or sewing machine), and a seam ripper.

Hand or machine stitch a line on the fabric. The fabric is the affected part of the patient, whether physical or otherwise. The thread is the illness, having bound itself to the patient. Use the point of a seam ripper to pick apart the seam rather than cutting through it. Take care not to break the thread as you work. The thread is the illness, easing away and leaving behind the fabric—and patient—whole. Bury the thread in the earth. It is done.

BUTTON MAGICK

Buttons weren't used as fasteners until the thirteenth century; however, they were in use for thousands of years before then as ornamentation. Sewing on a button is one of the first lessons taught, and it's a skill by which many people rate their competency at "adulting" (right along with being able to make their own doctor's appointment and cooking a meal more complicated than heating up a can of soup). Buttons are seen both as necessary (most shirts and other articles of clothing come with extra buttons for repairs) and as extraneous (the cookie tin filled with random buttons is standard in many homes). All of this is to say that buttons lend themselves to spellwork and talismans.

Most of the spells that follow create talismans that are meant to be worn. If you want to keep your button charms secret, you can keep them instead in a special spell pouch or box on your altar and only bring them out to add extra energy to your spells. Another option is to charm a single button and then sew it into the inside hem of an article of clothing. However you choose to use the spells, enjoy the creativity that goes into picking the right buttons. You will most likely end up, like so many other sewists, with a jar or tin of loose buttons ready to be used at a moment's notice.

Charm for Faithful Love

Take two red buttons and place them back to back. These represent you and your love. Using red thread, sew them together. As you sew, say,

> *By thread and knot,*
> *We will never part.*

Tie off the thread and place the charm somewhere safe where it can work its magick on you and your love (the bedroom, for example).

To Prevail in Legal Matters

Glue an orange button to a large metal paper clip. Use a small square of black or brown felt on the other side to help secure the glue and button. Say,

> *My cause is just, my cause is right,*
> *I will win this legal fight.*

Use the paper clip on your legal documents.

To Counter a Tendency to Lose Items

Take a found button. With three strands of purple thread, sew it to a 3" × 3" piece of cotton while saying,

> *Lost to me no more,*
> *I find all that I seek.*

Carry your new talisman with you in your pocket, purse, or satchel. When you have misplaced or forgotten something, hold the talisman in your receptive hand and repeat the saying while focusing on the item. The lost item will soon be revealed to you.

Talisman for Self-Love

Gather seven buttons of varying sizes and in various shades of pink. You can also add charms or beads that represent love: heart-shaped beads, charms with the word "love" on them, and so on.

Using beading wire, string the charms, beads, and buttons, running the wire through one hole of the buttons and then back through another. Twist the wire together at the top of the charm and make a loop.

Hold the charm in both hands and ground and center yourself. Breathe deeply, pulling in love and light and pushing out any negative self-thoughts. With each in-breath think of all the qualities and traits that you love about yourself, all the things that make you a unique individual. Continue until you are full to bursting with feelings of love. Bring the charm up to your heart and say,

From feet to belly to heart to crown, I love myself.

Feel love pouring from your heart into the charm.

String the charm onto a chain or ribbon and wear it. When you need a reminder that you are worthy of love, hold the charm in your hand and feel the gentle glow of love that is stored in it.

Money and Prosperity Bracelets

Pick six or nine buttons. Choose large—1" or larger—shankless buttons with four holes for this charm. Pick buttons in green, silver, or gold. Use hemp rope in shades of brown or green.

1 Thread the ends of the rope through two holes of the four-hole button. Leave a small bit of the rope at the back of the button to form a loop.

2 Cross the ends of the rope, feeding them back through the other two holes so that the rope makes an X on the front.

3 Pull both ends of the rope through the loop, pulling on the rope to tighten the loop until the excess is taken up.

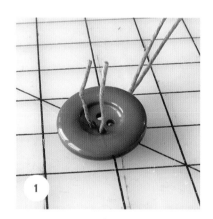

Threading the rope ends through the loop and tightening it creates the toggle for the bracelet closure.

4   Thread the rope through the rest of the buttons, leaving three inches of the rope empty. Make a loop at the end of the rope to fit over the first button.

5   Don the bracelet and say,

> *Penny by penny, pound by pound,*
> *Prosperity pours into my hands.*

6   Visualize green-, silver-, and gold-tinted energy radiating from the bracelet and pulling prosperity to you.

Wear the bracelet when you are engaged in money-making endeavors: working, interviewing for a job, attending conferences, and so on.

When It Isn't Coming Together

Keep your goal in mind as you work and be aware you may run into obstacles. The thread might tangle in your sewing machine. You might attach a sleeve inside out. You may run out of piping two inches from the end. Don't let these problems discourage you. Pause, take a breath, and center yourself. If that isn't enough for you to return to the flow of your work, go through the following suggestions:

CHECK IN WITH YOURSELF

When you find yourself growing frustrated with your work, check in with yourself. When you've had to rethread your machine three times now and you are cursing with each stitch, take a step back. Is your heart really into the work right now? Are you pushing yourself to finish something when you really would rather be doing something else? Are you hungry? Thirsty? Are you getting sick?

Working magick when you aren't completely present is never a good idea. At best, your project will fall apart and not work the way you had intended. Oh, the physical item might be all right, but the magick will sputter and fail. At worst, the magick will backfire, tainted by the annoyance it picked up as you were working.

Be honest with yourself, and if you find that you just aren't in the right frame of mind to be working magick, walk away. Your magick self is trying to send you a message, and you need to heed it.

CHECK IN WITH YOUR TOOLS

Maybe you jumped into the sewing session without checking out your tools beforehand. Does your sewing machine need a cleaning or oiling? Are your scissors in need of sharpening? Stop what you are doing, take a few centering breaths, and then go over your tools. Make sure they aren't sending you a message that they need attention. Better to cut your sewing session short and take care of your things than try to push through and end up with something flawed that doesn't work.

CHECK IN WITH YOUR ENVIRONMENT

Maybe it's not you but your workspace that is throwing a monkey wrench in your work. Especially if your workspace shares room with other things (you set up at the kitchen table, for example), the vibrations and intentions from others might have crept into the area. Smudge your work area with sage or incense. Sweep the area with a besom or ring a bell.

CHECK FOR OUTSIDE INFLUENCES

If you've ruled out physical and environmental issues, it's time to check in with the supernatural. The best way to keep negative magickal influences from your work is to prepare ahead of time with your circle casting. Sometimes that isn't enough, however, and it's time to take more active protective measures.

GREMLINS, HOBS, AND OTHER MISCHIEVOUS SPIRITS

If I had a dollar for every time I lost my scissors or tape measure or other tool, I would have a stack of money I couldn't find. Living in a house with two children and my own forgetfulness usually is the reason things go missing; however, I am certain our house gnomes are responsible for many a missing seam ripper.

When I find myself searching for a ruler and the kids swear up and down they haven't taken it, I try this simple folk charm: I clap my hands three times and call out what I am looking for. The house gnomes sometimes take the hint and set the missing item out where I looked just minutes before.

If you suspect fae are responsible for your work going pear-shaped, you can ward your workspace to keep them from entering. Iron (such as a horseshoe or even nails) can be hung above the entrance or above the space. Bells also are effective against fae mischief. Mistletoe hung over your workspace will also keep fae away.

Keep in mind, if a house gnome or gremlin is mucking about in your work, repelling them will only set their attentions to other areas of your home. It might be wise to make a peace offering of food and drink to make up for banishing them from your workspace. Some alcohol or cake left out would help soothe any hurt feelings the displaced fae might harbor.

It is worth noting that faeries expect any home or work environment they encounter to be neat and tidy. So if you are finding your threads tangled, your scissors missing, or your needles breaking, you might want to check and make sure your workplace isn't driving any workshop helpers or passing faeries to act out.

For more generalized banishing of negativity, smudge your workspace with sage. If you have a room where you sew, mix cumin and salt together and then sprinkle it on the windowsills and the doorway to stop evil from entering. Or try this charm:

In a pouch made of black cloth add a piece of quartz, salt, and cloves. Charge the pouch by saying,

All evil stay away from me, all evil leave me be, all evil let me work in peace.

Hang the pouch over your workspace.

You can also keep a basil, ivy, or cactus plant near your workspace to dispel evil.

Magickal

Crafts

For the Altar

I have yet to encounter a religion that doesn't make use of an altar. That doesn't mean there aren't any, of course. However, there is a strong likelihood that whatever your path, you maintain some kind of altar. And where there are altars there is the need for dressing them. The following projects cover a range of altar cloths and bowls for offering.

An altar cloth is one of the simplest and most versatile pieces of an altar. It can be easy to overlook this piece of equipment because it is covered by all the other tools of the craft. However, altar cloths act as the foundation for altars. They carve a magick space out of a mundane surface. Power is held in their boundaries. Through their materials and decoration, they set the tone for ritual. And altar cloths for each sabbat and esabbat can help usher in the different energies found in the Wheel of the Year.

Making your own altar cloth doesn't have to be expensive or complicated. A trip to your local fabric store will give you many options in the quilting aisles, especially seasonal prints. If you are a thrifty shopper, you can even check out the sale fabric right after a major holiday to stock up on prints for next year. For a no-sew option, measure the area of your altar, cut out the fabric to that size, and you are done. You can cut the edges with pinking shears to avoid fraying. If you have twenty minutes or more, you can make a narrow hem by turning the edges into the wrong side of the fabric ¼" and then again another ¼". Sew a seam around the entire hem and you're done.

Take time to plan out what you want to do; think about fabric and color choices. Browse the trim aisles and think about what you could do to add more layers of meaning and magick. When you are finished, you'll have an altar cloth that evokes a sense of wonder that will aid you in your spellcasting and ritual work.

Simple Square Altar Cloth

MATERIALS
1¼ yards of 44" wide quilting cotton
Thread

DIFFICULTY
✂ ✂ ✂

TIME
1 hour

Some of the projects in this chapter make use of store-bought tablecloths. You can also make your own square cloth following the instructions here.

1 Wash, dry, and press fabric. (See page 75 for laundry wash suggestions.)

2 Hem all four sides of the fabric with a standard hem. Your altar cloth is now ready for embellishment.

1 Fold the fabric in half once and then in half again. Pin through all layers of fabric along the edges.

2 Place a yardstick against the center seam corner. Measure 21½" from the corner to the edge of the fabric. Pivot the ruler a couple of inches and make another mark 21½" from the corner. Continue to pivot and mark until you have made markings from one corner to another of the fabric. If you don't have a yardstick, cut a length of string 21½". Use a pin or thumbtack to secure one end of the string to the corner. Lay the string along the edge of the fabric and mark where it ends. Pivot the string as for the yardstick.

3 Draw a line across all the markings, creating a quarter circle. Cut along the line and unfold the altar cloth.

4 Topstitch a line ¼" away from the edge of the altar cloth. This creates a guide around the edges of the altar cloth that helps you achieve a smooth curve. Fold and press the edge of the cloth to the wrong side along the stitching. Fold again.

5 Topstitch around the whole edge of the altar cloth.

Simple Circle Altar Cloth

MATERIALS
Chalk, pen, or pencil for marking
Yardstick
1¼ yards of 44" wide quilting cotton
Thread

DIFFICULTY
✂ ✂ ✂

TIME
1 hour

A circular altar cloth takes only a few more steps than the square altar cloth. Wash, dry, and iron the fabric before sewing.

Don't stress about drawing a perfect curve.

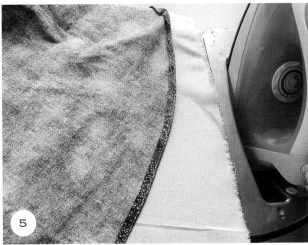

Elemental Altar Runner

- - - - - - - - - - - - - - - - - - -

MATERIALS

2 pieces of fabric, 9" × 18", in green,
yellow, red, and blue, for a total of
8 pieces
1 piece of black or white fabric, 9" × 18",
for the center
2 rectangles of white or black fabric,
37" × 18", for the backing
Thread
Four tassels in gold or silver

DIFFICULTY

TIME

2 hours

*Not all altars are square or round tables. My
family altar is set up on a coffee table. For
those times when you need a rectangular altar cloth, make the Elemental Altar Runner.
It can be made with cotton in solid colors.
You can also look for prints that combine
the colors with elemental symbols: a green
floral print for earth, a yellow print with a
swirl design for air, a red flame print for fire,
and a blue wave print for water, for example. Not all paths use the above color correspondences, so feel free to substitute the
recommended color combinations for those
of your practice.*

1 Wash, dry, and iron the fabric.

2 With right sides together, sew the pieces together along the long sides in this order: green
to yellow, yellow to red, red to blue. Use a ½"
seam. Pinning the fabric all together before
sewing can help keep the pieces in order. Repeat with the remaining color fabric.

3 Sew the blue piece of one color band to the
center piece, right sides together, using a ½"
seam. Repeat on the other side.

4 Press all the seams open.

5 Sew the backing fabric together along the
short sides with a ½" seam. Press the seam
open.

6 Tack the tassels to each corner of the runner,
with the tassels facing toward the inside.
When you turn the altar cloth right-side out,
they will hang from the corners.

7 With right sides together, sew the runner
backing to the runner along all sides using a
½" seam. Leave a 3" gap for turning, and be
careful not to catch the tassels in the seam.
Trim the corners.

8 Turn the runner right-side out. Using a chopstick or turning tool, carefully push out the
corners. Press the runner.

9 Topstitch around all the edges of the runner,
closing the gap used for turning.

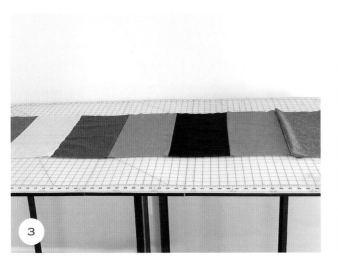

Bias Binding Pentacle Altar Cloth

- -

MATERIALS

Premade tablecloth

2 packages of ¼" double-folded bias
   binding (4 yards each) in color of your
   choice

DIFFICULTY

TIME

2 hours

*This altar cloth takes advantage of bias bind-
ing's flexible nature to create one of the most
familiar symbols of modern Paganism: the
pentacle. Use the instructions here to embellish a premade altar cloth or tablecloth.*

1. Using tracing paper, copy the pentacle design
   on pages 224–27.

2. Find and mark the center of the tablecloth.

3. Using transfer paper, transfer the design onto
   the cloth at its center.

4. Starting at the top point of the pentagram,
   sew the bias binding along the line running
   down to the bottom left point.

5. Flip the bias binding over at the point and sew
   up along the line running to the right upper
   point.

6. Continue sewing the pentagram. Backstitch at
   the end point to secure it. Clip the excess bias
   binding.

7. Starting at the top point of the pentagram,
   sew the bias binding along the line of the circle. Backstitch at the overlap when you reach
   the top again to secure the bias binding. Clip
   the excess.

USE A
LIGHT-COLORED
TRANSFER PAPER
OR PEN TO TRACE
THE DESIGN.

Fold the binding at the point of the pentacle before you reach it and then pivot at the point.

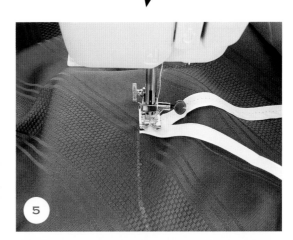

INSTRUCTIONS ON HOW TO MAKE THE FABRIC TWINE USED IN THESE BOWLS CAN BE FOUND ON PAGE 198. THIS IS A GOOD WEEKEND PROJECT: MAKE YOUR TWINE ONE DAY AND MAKE THE BASKETS THE NEXT.

1 Take one end of the fabric twine and roll it in on itself to make a starting spiral, like a little snail. *If machine sewing:* Place this first small spiral under the presser foot of your sewing machine. Position the spiral so that the free end of the fabric twine falls to the right of the spiral. *If hand sewing:* Hold the starting spiral in your non-dominant hand.

2 *If machine sewing:* Set your sewing machine to a zigzag stitch. Stitch back and forth over the starting spiral a couple of times to anchor it. *If hand sewing:* Sew several stitches across the starting spiral to secure it from coming undone.

3 *If machine sewing:* Start sewing, making sure the needle catches the starting spiral and the twine you are feeding into it. Work slowly and carefully. *If hand sewing:* Continue the spiral, turning the spiral around and adding twine to the outside of the starting spiral. Bring the needle up through the starting spiral and down through the added twine. Continue, anchoring the new twine to the existing spiral.

4 Keep turning the spiral, feeding more twine, increasing the spiral as you go. Make five or six rotations to create the bottom. The base of your bowl determines how large it will be.

5 *If machine sewing:* Adjust the spiral so that it is at a 90-degree angle to the deck of the sewing machine. Keep stitching, forming the walls of the bowl. *If hand sewing:* Adjust the spiral so that it is at a 90-degree angle to the previous spiral. Continue stitching the new twine to the existing spiral, forming the walls of the bowl. Use one hand to bend the base of your bowl as you feed more twine into your needle.

6 Stitch slowly, being careful when you reach a join in the fabric twine. When machine sewing, you may have to grasp the bowl from behind the presser foot to help move it through

Altar Bowls

MATERIALS
3 yards fabric twine (see page 198) for a small bowl
Thread
Embroidery needle or sewing machine with a needle for thick fabrics

DIFFICULTY
✂ ✂ ✂

TIME
1 hour

Our household altar is set up on a coffee table in the living room (which we call "the library" because it is where the majority of our books are shelved), right in front of the windows that look out on the street. It is a sprawling affair, covered in rocks collected from various places, dried flowers from bouquets my children have brought me, pinecones, sticks, candles, feathers, and any number of items that rotate onto and off the space. Often I will place various materia magica on it in the lead-up to actually using them in ritual or spellwork. The whole thing can sometimes get out of hand, resembling less a sacred altar and more a magickal junk drawer. To corral some of the disorder, I have little bowls made from fabric twine.

Because they are made of fabric, they are lightweight. They are flexible, meaning they can sit flat. And while the bowls on my altar are small, fitting in the palm of my hand, they can be made into any size or shape, limited only by the amount of fabric twine and time you have.

Photos are shown on the next page.

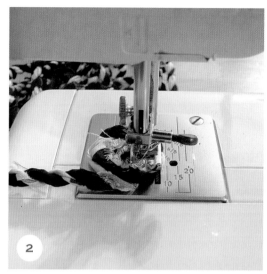

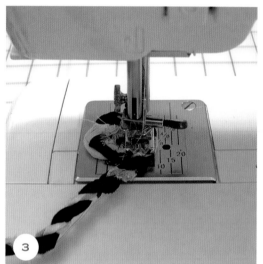

the feed dogs (the toothed piece below the presser foot that moves the fabric along).

7 When you get close to the end of the fabric twine, cut off the knot end. At the half of inch of the fabric twine, stitch back and forth a few times to anchor the end.

Experiment with various sizes and shapes of bowls. Make them as gifts for friends. Make one to hold your jewelry. Decorate the outsides with beads and buttons and charms. This is a project where you can let your creativity run wild.

Start your bowl by
curling the end like a snail.
The zigzag stitch holds your
tiny snail together.

THE SPIDER
PINCUSHION BRINGS
THE ENERGIES OF THE
MYTH OF ARACHNE
INTO YOUR SEWING
ROOM.

Instruments of Magick

$\mathcal{L}$ike crafting a wand or scrying mirror, making your own sewing tools forges a personal connection between you and the implements of sewing spellcraft. That relationship can often add to the success of any magickal endeavors.

In this section you'll find practical tools, such as the Spider Pincushion on page 106, and also magickal helpers, such as the Sewing Poppet on page 108 and the House Gnomes on page 113.

Do not be afraid to change up these projects. Choose different colored fabric and use buttons and trims that have a connection to you. Yarn is suggested as hair for the Sewing Poppet, but you could substitute ribbons, embroidery thread, or fabric scraps, or skip the hair entirely. These are meant to be aids for you, and personalization will only make them more helpful in your sewing magick.

Spider Pincushion

- -

MATERIALS
¼ yard muslin
Thread
8 ounces emery or crushed walnut shells
¼ yard black wool
Scraps of black felt for the legs
Small black beads for the eyes

DIFFICULTY

TIME
1 hour

Even if, like me, you have a fear of spiders, you might find a place in your sewing space for this little Spider Pincushion. Spiders, with their natural weaving ability, are linked with fiber arts all over the world. "People across West Africa attributed their spinning skills to Ananse, a spider deity. In North America, a Hopi spider goddess was believed to spin and weave cotton," Sven Beckert writes in his book Empire of Cotton. *This association makes the spider well suited for holding, sharpening, and blessing your pins and needles.*

Emery is a material composed of superfine particles and used in commercial pincushions. It sharpens pins and needles as they are pushed into the pincushion. It can be bought online or from specialty craft stores. Look for packages marked "emery sand." Ground walnut shells can also be used, as they have the same sharpening properties. They can be found online or in pet stores, where they are sold as reptile bedding.

Wool is used in this project because the lanolin in it is believed to help keep pins and needles rust free.

1 Using tracing paper, trace the pattern pieces for the interior, body, and legs on page 228.

2 Cut out 2 circles from the muslin. With wrong sides together, sew a ¼" seam around the circles, leaving a space for filling.

3 Fill the circles with emery or ground walnut shells (a funnel is recommended). Fill as full as possible.

4 Hand baste the opening closed with small stitches. Test your basting by giving the interior a shake or two. If any filling leaks out, add extra stitches.

5 Cut out 2 circles from the black wool.

6 Cut out 8 leg pieces from the black felt.

7 Tack the legs to the right side of one circle at dots with the rounded edge to the inside. Sew in place. When you turn the body right-side out, the legs will extend to the outside.

8 Add eyes to the right side of the other circle by sewing on the beads.

9 With right sides together, sew a ¼" seam around the spider's body. Leave an opening large enough to slip in the interior emery bag.

10 Turn the body right-side out.

11 Insert the emery bag. Slip stitch the opening closed.

CHARGING
Burn a pine incense, either one you've made yourself or store-bought. Facing east, waft the pincushion through the smoke and say,

Spider weaving your web wide,
I place my pins and needles inside.
Keep them sharp and keep them safe.
Keep them always in their place.

EMBROIDERY CAN ALSO BE USED TO MAKE THE SPIDER'S EYES.

Sewing Poppet

MATERIALS
½ yard muslin
Craft-weight interfacing
Thread
Embroidery thread
Polyester stuffing
Yarn (optional)
Metal washer (optional)

DIFFICULTY

TIME
2 hours

Poppets have been used in magick for centuries. They have been made from roots, wood, clay, metal, and rags, and have served various purposes, from sympathetic spellwork to aiding witches in their magick. Poppets can be vaguely humanlike or intricately detailed to represent a particular person, depending on their purpose and the skill and needs of their creators.

The poppet projects in this book tap into that long history. You can make a poppet to aid you while you work, one to help keep your mind magickally uncluttered, or one to serve solely as a pincushion.

Create a poppet to hold your sewing tools or to sit on your altar. Fill her with herbs and crystals corresponding with your intent when working on a project and have her help you as you work.

1 Using tracing paper, trace the pattern pieces for the body, pocket, and bottom on pages 229–31.

2 Cut out 2 body pieces, 2 pocket pieces, and 1 bottom piece from fabric. Cut 1 bottom piece out of the craft-weight interfacing.

3 Sew the pocket pieces together along the top edge using a ¼" seam. Clip the curves so the pocket lies flat. Turn right-side out and press.

4 Place the pocket against the front body piece at the X marks, right sides together, matching the bottom edges. Baste along unfinished sides. Once you have basted the pocket to the front body, treat them as one piece of fabric.

5 Place the body pieces with right sides together. Sew with a ¼" seam, leaving the bottom open. Clip curves.

6 Fuse the interfacing to the wrong side of the bottom piece, following the interfacing directions.

7 With right sides together, sew the bottom onto the body, leaving a 3" opening to turn. Pin the bottom piece to the body in four places to keep everything in order. Remove the pins as you come to them while sewing.

8 Turn the poppet right-side out.

9 Using embroidery thread, add a face to the poppet on the side where the pocket is. Add yarn hair if you wish. Attach the hair by sewing it into the seam ("stitch in the ditch") to avoid fabric puckering when you stuff your poppet. You can also use pens, paints, or other craft items to make the face.

10 Stuff the poppet through the opening, making sure not to over-stuff it. If you wish, put a heavy washer at the bottom to give it weight and stability.

11 Stitch the opening closed using a slip stitch. Make sure you are sewing into the seam allowance of the bottom piece rather than trying to push the needle through the interfacing fused to the bottom.

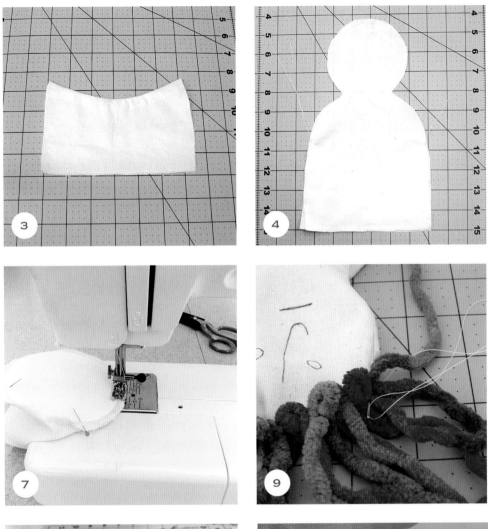

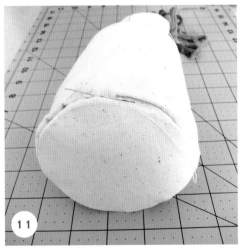

When finished, consecrate the poppet. Use the pocket to hold tools, or put in stones and herbs to amplify your work. Talk to your poppet as you sew, venting your frustrations, asking for help, or just keeping up a friendly commentary. Make sure to keep your poppet free of dust and dirt and set it in a place that gets adequate light.

Put a Pin in It Poppet

MATERIALS

7½" × 13½" piece of muslin

Thread

Embroidery thread, pens, buttons, or other notions to make a face

Polyester stuffing

1 teaspoon dried catnip for binding the intrusive thoughts (alternatively, use black pepper, cayenne pepper, cloves, dragon's blood, or pine)

1 teaspoon dried gardenia for a peaceful mind (alternatively, use lavender, meadowsweet, passion flower, vervain, or violet)

1 teaspoon of dried jasmine to increase the success of the binding (alternatively, use cedar, cinnamon, clover, ginger, lemon balm, or orange bergamot)

DIFFICULTY

✂ ✂ ✂

TIME

1 hour

The saying "put a pin in it" means to set aside a thought or idea to be revisited later. Although the original meaning of the phrase comes from WWII and was in reference to hand grenades, it can be used today in conjunction with a poppet for the following bit of sympathetic crafting magick.

I am a chronic worrier. I also deal with depression and anxiety, which means my brain is constantly bombarded with intrusive thoughts. They are unwanted visitors that don't respect my boundaries and like to play "what if?" games that are anything but fun. The worst part? Most of these concerns are about things that will never happen or things I have no control over. And yet, despite how disruptive these thought patterns are, they manage to sneak past my metaphorical brain bouncer and wreak havoc.

I have found one way to ease some of the unpleasantness is to work a bit of magick and make the immaterial material. I magickally pin those intrusive thoughts onto a specially made poppet. This is a type of binding spell like the one mentioned on page 79, but it allows for you to release the thought should you wish or have need to later.

1   Using tracing paper, trace the pattern piece for the body on page 232. Cut the pattern out.

2   Fold the muslin in half for a double thickness. Pin the edges.

3   Trace the pattern onto the fabric.

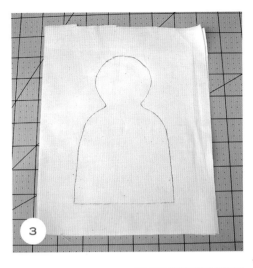

4   Sew on top of the outline from point A to point B. Remember to backstitch at the start and end of the seam. Pivot on tight corners by leaving the needle in the fabric, lifting the presser foot, and then physically turning the fabric to where it needs to be. Lower the presser foot and continue sewing.

5   Cut around the seam about ⅛" away from it. Clip curves and trim corners so that your poppet has the correct shape when turned right-side out and stuffed.

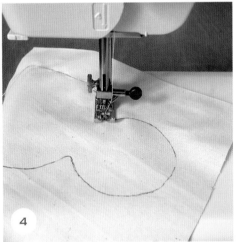

6   Turn poppet right-side out. Use a chopstick or other turning tool to push out corners and curves.

No need to pin a pattern for this project. You'll be sewing on the lines you've traced.

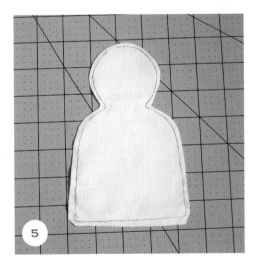

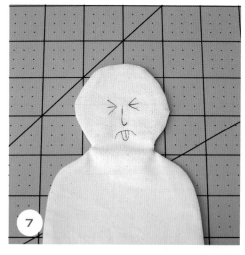

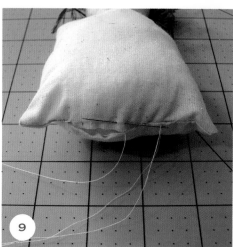

7 Embroider, ink, paint, or use other materials to give your poppet a face. You can also give it hair.

8 In a bowl, mix your chosen herbs. Fill the poppet with the herbs and then fill with stuffing.

9 Using a slip stitch, close the opening. Adding a closing flourish as you stitch such as "It is done" or "As I will it" gives your spellwork a sense of finality.

When you are troubled by thoughts that won't leave you alone—nagging worries, concerns over things you can't control, etc.—take a pin and stick it in the poppet. Say,

Here I pin you and here you stay, not to be released until I say.

See the bothersome thought being stuck through with the pin and secured to the poppet as you push the pin in. If, at a later time, the thought attempts to intrude again, visualize it once again stuck to the poppet.

When you are ready to deal with the thought or concern, simply pull out the pin and say,

I release you.

ALTERNATE USE

A pincushion can be made from this poppet as well. Use a slightly heavier cloth, like quilting cotton or broadcloth. Omit the herbs and replace the stuffing with crushed walnut shells or emery so that your pins will be sharpened when they are pushed into the poppet.

Before you first use your poppet pincushion, charge it with the task of keeping your needles and pins sharp. Turn it over and anoint the back with an oil aligned with your sewing objectives, such as clary sage for creativity in sewing or rose for the transformative process of sewing. As you anoint the poppet, say,

In they go,
Sharp as wit;
Out they come,
Ready to stitch.

Sewing creates a lot of waste: fabric remnants, snippets of thread, blunted needles. As a Pagan, a witch, and a citizen of the world, I have a hard time throwing anything out that I can find a use for. Fortunately, most of it is recyclable. The following project takes some of that waste and uses it to further your magickal sewing.

Empty spools of thread can also be used in various craft projects. The long cones of serger thread especially lend themselves to the following project, although regular spools can be used as well.

Create your own house gnomes to help with your sewing. Because they are so small, they only require scraps, so they'll use up a lot of your leftovers. They also make wonderful gifts for Yule and winter celebrations.

House Gnomes

MATERIALS
Old sock, old sweater, or yarn
Hot glue gun
Empty spools of thread
Wool felt
Black, brown, or pink beads

DIFFICULTY
✄ ✄ ✄

TIME
15 minutes

1 Cut the sock or sweater down to fit ¾ of the height of the spool. Hot glue the material to the spool, making sure it covers the bottom of the spool. If you are using yarn, wrap the spool ¾ of the way up from the bottom, using hot glue at intervals to hold it in place.

2 Cut a triangle with a rounded bottom out of the felt. The bottom must be long enough to wrap around the top of the spool. Using hot glue, make the triangle into a gnome hat.

3 Place the hat on the spool, using hot glue to secure it. The hat should come down enough to cover the fabric or yarn so the spool does not show.

It's okay to cut the felt larger than you need; excess can be trimmed away.

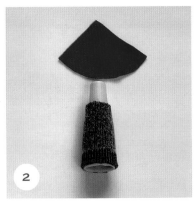

4 Glue the bead on for the nose. Position it so the hole faces up and down, rather than side to side.

5 If using a sock with an insulated interior, you can add a beard by pulling the sock down underneath the bead nose to show the inside. Trim the "beard" into shape.

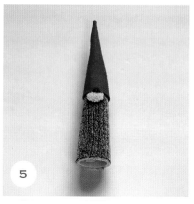

Once you have finished, charge your gnome or gnomes. Ask them to aid you in your sewing work, to protect your workshop and space, and to intercede with any other spirits who might take off with your tools. Set the gnome near your sewing altar or around your house.

You can also fill your gnome with stones or herbs, stopping up the bottom with a circular piece of cardboard, to enhance their magickal help. Any stones or herbs related to earth magick are suitable for the house gnomes and their magick, as they are associated with the earth. Ask them to lend their stability and practicality to any projects that are related to the household, wealth, or abundance.

Gnomes like luscious, non-wicking beards and hats that cover their eyes.

The tiny travel sewing kits that one can get from gas stations and dollar stores can be useful in a pinch. However, they leave a lot to be desired for the sewist and witch who needs to be able to sew on the go. Dragging around a well-stocked sewing basket isn't an ideal solution. The witches I know already haul around oversized bags filled with notebooks, pens, novels, snacks, jars and baggies full of herbs, crystals, sunglasses, lip balm, and scarves. For the sake of our aching backs, there needs to be an in-between option.

The Travel Sewing Kit is my compromise. It has space to hold a pair of detail scissors, a standard tape measure, and three bobbins of thread. It also has a deep pocket for buttons, safety pins, or other small notions. The pocket flap serves as a place to keep pins and needles.

It is made out of felt to keep the construction as simple as possible. Try to use wool felt rather than polyester if you can, as it stands up to the pressing needed in the later steps. The heavy-weight craft interfacing gives the kit stability and some protection for the tools and notions within.

This is a project that lends itself to personalization. Add buttons and other embellishments to the cover. Use a whip stitch for the edges. Choose different colors of wool felt.

Travel Sewing Kit

MATERIALS
1 piece of green felt, 8½" × 7", plus scraps for pockets
1 piece of gray felt, 8½" × 7"
¾" elastic
Elastic cord
1 piece of heavy-weight fusible craft interfacing, 8½" × 7"
Button

DIFFICULTY

TIME
1 hour

1   Using tracing paper, trace the pattern pieces for the kit on page 233: 1 gray rectangle, 1 green rectangle, 1 rectangular pocket, 1 pocket flap, and 1 scissors pocket.

2   Cut the green and gray rectangles. Cut out the scissor and pocket pattern pieces from the scraps of green felt.

3   Cut one 1¼" piece of the ¾" elastic for the tape measure holder. Cut one 3½" piece of the ¾" elastic for the bobbin holder. Cut one 2½" piece of the elastic cord for the closure.

4   Position the scissor pocket on the interior felt piece as indicated on the pattern. Sew a scant ⅛" around the curved edge of the pocket, backstitching at the start and finish. Sew again ¼" around the curved edge.

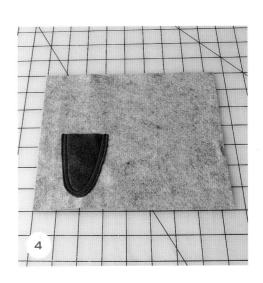

5   Position the pocket piece as indicated on the pattern. Sew a scant ⅛" around the right, bottom, and left sides of the pocket, leaving the top open. Backstitch at the start and finish. Sew again ¼" around the three sides.

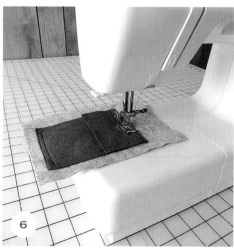

6   Pick one side of the pocket flap piece to be the "right side" of the fabric. Position the pocket flap piece right-side down above the flap indicated on the pattern, the bottom of the felt aligned with top edge of the flap. The flap piece will extend away from the pocket. Sew ⅛" along the edge closest to the pocket. Backstitch at the start and finish. Fold the flap down on this seam so that it covers the pocket. Sew ¼" from the top of the fold, encasing the first seam, and remember to backstitch at the start and finish.

7   Position the tape measure elastic as indicated on the pattern. Sew a scant ⅛" along each raw edge several times to anchor it and keep it from fraying.

The flap not only serves to keep items in the pocket secure but also acts as a place to store needles and pins.

THE BACKSTITCHING AND MULTIPLE LINES OF STITCHING ARE NECESSARY TO ENSURE THE KIT CAN HOLD UP TO LOTS OF HANDLING.

8 To make the bobbin holder, position the bobbin elastic as indicated on the pattern. Sew a scant ⅛" along each raw edge several times to anchor it. Sew 1" away from the right edge seam of the elastic. Sew several times. Repeat 1" away from the left edge.

9 Make a loop of the elastic cord. Tack it to the wrong side of the interior felt piece by stitching along the right edge 3½" from the top edge. Make sure the ends of the elastic loop are on the wrong side of the interior felt piece so they don't show in the finished kit.

10 Place the exterior felt piece right-side down. Position the interfacing in the center of the felt. Place the interior felt piece right-side up on top of the interfacing. Using a press cloth, press all the layers of the travel kit, fusing the interfacing to both pieces of felt. Press both sides of the travel kit.

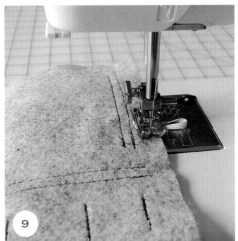

Use a press cloth to make sure you don't scorch the felt. If you are using a polyester felt, a press cloth is necessary to keep the felt from melting.

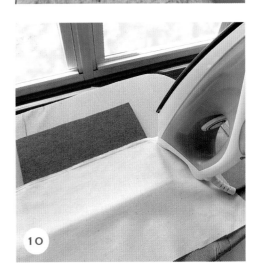

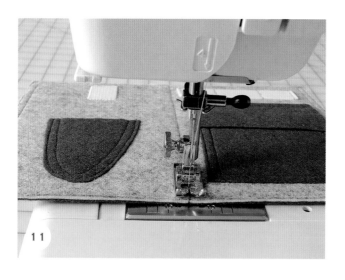

11 Using a heavy-duty needle, topstitch ⅛" all around the edge of the kit. Stitch again ¼" around all edges. Mark a line 4¼" down the center of the travel kit. Topstitch along this line to create a fold line, allowing the kit to fold like a book.

12 Attach the button on the outside of the travel kit, 3½" from the top edge. Fold the travel kit closed and loop the elastic cord over the button.

1. Cut a 7" × 7" square of fabric. Increase the size of the fabric square by 1" if you are adding large stones or objects to the pattern weight. Pinking shears can be used to reduce fraying at the edges.

2. Place 2 tablespoons of rice into the middle of the square and then bring the corners and edges up.

3. The customization comes in with the filling of the pattern weight. You can add herbs or crystals that correspond with your purpose to focus your magickal intent. Add a penny to pattern weights when you are working on a project for abundance, prosperity, or money spells. A piece of agate or carnelian can be nestled in with the rice to add protective properties. A sprinkle of therapeutic herbs such as mullein or hyssop can enhance healing projects.

4. Secure the edges with a rubber band. You have now made a pattern weight that can be easily placed and moved.

Pattern Weight

MATERIALS
Fabric of your choice
Rice
Rubber bands

DIFFICULTY

TIME
15 minutes

Pattern weights are used when you are tracing a pattern directly onto fabric. In my workshop, I occasionally use two bookends in the shape of Oxford bobbies (their names are Nigel and Trevor). However, you can buy or make your own weights in the event that you don't have a couple of your own bobbies on hand.

Making pattern weights is as easy as picking up ¾" washers from a home improvement store. You can use them as is or paint them, wrap them in ribbon or yarn, or even dip them in the rubberizing coating used for tools.

I find washers to be a bit difficult to use because I have a hard time picking them up to move them. Also, as I wrote on page 12 about using pinhead colors to enhance your sewing magick, I prefer to be able to match tools to magickal intentions as often as possible. To that end, I came up with another way to create pattern weights that is cheap, easy, no-sew, and customizable.

THE TRICKSTER
SCARF IS A RANDOM,
FREEFORM ACCESSORY
MEANT TO TAP INTO
MODERN ENERGIES
OF CHAOS AND
CHANGE.

Magick to Wear

Cloth has had a long history in magickal practice in both its presence—ceremonial robes worn by priests of various paths—and its absence—the sky-clad Wiccans who abandon clothes for certain rituals. Beyond magickal garb, however, clothing and magick have been interwoven since ancient times. When Romans had their clothes stolen, they would respond with curse tablets. In his book *The Devil's Cloth*, Michel Pastoureau notes, "Aren't our pajamas striped to protect us during the night, while we rest, fragile and pathetic, from all bad dreams and interventions by the devil?"

Even today, clothes can indicate status, profession, manner, interests, and disposition. It is no wonder that old love divinations often sought an image of one's future beloved in the clothes they wore every day. Clothing is an intimate part of us and can be treated as an extension of the physical body in magick. Healing charms call for a piece of the patient's clothing, or a piece of cloth wiped against the patient's brow can be used. A piece of shirt is used in a voodoo doll to make a sympathetic connection with the victim. Even the magician's top hat evokes the idea of magick before a rabbit is pulled out of it.

Clothing works everyday magick just in the way it can affect our moods—when we wear a favorite outfit, when our clothes itch, when what we wear is ill-fitting. When we want to express ourselves, we turn to our clothes.

There are many ways you can add magick to your clothes, whether they are off the rack or handmade. Laundry rinses mentioned on page 76 can imbue your clothes with the magick essences of certain herbs. Or you can add witch stitches, as outlined on page 71, to your clothing. The following projects are accessories you can make for both mundane and ritual wear.

Glamour Scarf

MATERIALS
2 pieces of A fabric, 9" × 15"
2 pieces of B fabric, 9" × 15"
2 pieces of C fabric, 9" × 15"
2 pieces of D fabric, 9" × 15"
1 piece of E fabric, 9" × 15"
Color-coordinating thread

DIFFICULTY

TIME
1 hour

While glamour spells are well known in fiction and pseudo-historical accounts, the practical witch knows that she doesn't need exotic ingredients and a cauldron to amp up her allure. Makeup, jewelry, and clothing have all been used for millennia to increase the mystique of the wearer. With that in mind, make this scarf to wear when you need a boost of self-confidence and to add to your personal glamour.

For this project choose silks, brocades, fancy quilting cottons—anything that speaks glamour to you. Choose colors that appeal to you. Don't worry if the colors don't "suit" you according to some style guide. You are looking for colors and designs that make you happy. This is one project where synthetic materials are well suited, as they have properties associated with shape changing, illusion, and transformation. So feel free to add some polyester, acetate, acrylic, or other synthetic blends to your scarf.

For the thread, pick one color that coordinates with your chosen fabric. To amplify and refine your magickal intent, choose a shade from one of the color suggestions below.

Red or **yellow** for self-esteem
White for warding off doubts and fears
Orange for breaking down barriers
Green for changing directions or attitudes
Blue for self-improvement
Pink for self-love

1   With right sides together, sew the long sides of the fabric together with ½" seams in this order: A to B, B to C, and C to D. Repeat with the other A through D. Sew one fabric band to E. Sew the second band to the other side of choice E. Press the seams open.

2   On the outside, topstitch ¼" away from either side of the seam.

3   Fold the long rectangle in half, right-side in, long sides together. Pin at every seam to secure the fabric from shifting while you sew.

4   Sew a ½" seam along one short and one long side. Turn the scarf right-side out through the open short end. Fold the unfinished edges of the open end ½" inward and press to keep them in place until you sew them closed.

5   Topstitch ¼" from the edge around the entire length of the scarf, closing the opening.

The outside edge of most presser feet is ¼" from the needle, making it a handy guide for topstitching.

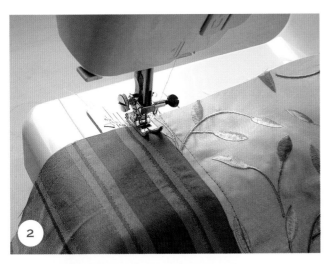

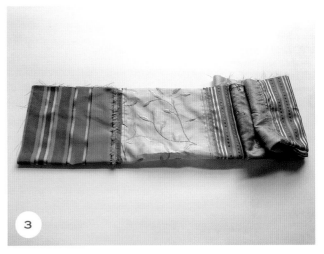

CHARGING

Take your newly sewn scarf and an ounce of chocolate (or other treat that you find decadent) and stand before a full-length mirror. If you wish, put on music that puts you in the mood of glamour and magick.

As you stand before the mirror, put on the scarf. Admire how you look. See the glamour magick imbued in the scarf shimmering in a gold-white light that extends to encompass your entire body. Call upon a god or goddess of beauty, love, or magick (perhaps Aphrodite, Eros, Ishtar, or another deity that you associate with those properties) by saying,

I call upon you, [deity].
I am seen as I want to be seen.
I am seen as beautiful, confident, and successful [substitute with the attributes you desire].
They only see what I want them to see.

Take a bite of the chocolate as you watch yourself in the mirror, seeing the beautiful, confident, successful person you are reflected back to you. Wear the scarf whenever you need an extra boost to your outward perception by others.

Topstitching around all the edges of the scarf gives it a finished look as well as closes the open end.

The circle is a symbol of completion, rebirth, cycles, and renewal. Each end leads into a beginning. It is also a symbol of protection. It marks a boundary between the safe interior and the unknown outside. It is how we delineate between the personal and the public.

And it is ultimately a symbol of protection. There is a reason practitioners of so many different Pagan paths cast a circle before working magick.

Sometimes your personal space can use a magickal boost. The world can be a crowded place. Catcallers, manspreaders, and hostile personalities can test your mental and emotional balance. Make yourself this cowl to create a physical boundary, allowing you to wrap yourself in its protection as you venture out into the world. It can hang down as a scarf, but when you need an extra boost of protection (or when it is cold outside) you can pull it up over your head.

Choose a fabric with protective qualities: colors such as black, white, purple, or pink and designs such as circles, dogs, hedgehogs, cactus, and ivy. The fabric you choose should feel nice to you. It will be touching the sensitive skin of your neck and head, after all. Heavy-weight fabrics are not suggested, as they'll be too bulky when worn. For a very quick cowl, choose a knit, as you can skip the steps on finishing the edges.

To enhance your working, add an infusion of bay, chamomile, mint, black pepper, thistle, or another protective herb to your initial wash of the fabric.

While you are sewing, envision the finished cowl creating a circle of protection around you. Nothing harmful or negative can pierce this circle.

Protective Cowl

MATERIALS
1 yard of 58" wide fabric
Thread

DIFFICULTY
✂ ✂ ✂

TIME
30 minutes

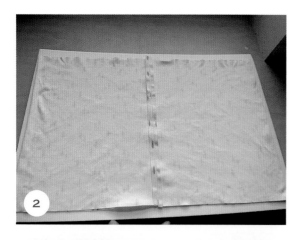

1 With right sides together, sew the short ends with a ½" seam.

2 Press the seam open. This helps reduce bulk.

3 On the right side of the fabric, edge stitch ¼" from the seam so that the edges on the wrong side are tacked down.

4 Make a narrow hem on both long edges of the circle.

CHARGING

Open the cowl out and lay it out on the floor. Sit inside the circle made of the cowl. Envision a circle of bright white light surrounding you and the cowl. The circle is a permeable barrier that you control. Nothing can enter that you don't allow, and any negativity or harmful energy cannot enter.

Envision the circle contracting, intensifying as it closes in around you and the cowl. Once the circle reaches the cowl, see it being absorbed by the fabric, imbuing it with the circle's protective qualities. Feel the gentle aura the cowl now gives off.

Don the cowl and head out into the world, knowing you are protected.

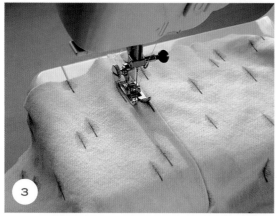

Hemming gives weight that adds a lovely drape to this scarf.

Trickster Scarf

MATERIALS

2 yards of water-soluble film stabilizer

Fabric scraps

Thread

DIFFICULTY

✂ ✂ ✂

TIME

2 hours

If I were asked to describe my aesthetic, it would be ridiculous skirts and graphic T-shirts. I am fond of mixing patterns and colors in ways that haven't been seen since the inside of a Victorian parlor. I like long, floofy skirts, even though the prevailing fashion advice of the day says they aren't flattering for my body type. I write this not to advertise how unfashionable I am but to point out that sometimes we need to ignore the "wisdom" of experts and wear what we damn well please. In a time when so many of us can't live the way we wish because of the constraints of money and society, being able to wear what makes us happy can be an act of rebellion that makes the other ways we have to conform bearable.

It is from this thought that the Trickster Scarf was born. Around the world, the Trickster is a being who upends social and gender norms. The Trickster bends words and rules—even breaks them at times. The Trickster wears pants when everyone else is wearing skirts, wears skirts when everyone is wearing pants, or goes completely nude just to remind us that clothing can be optional. The Trickster comes around asking, Why, why, why? All of this is a gift to us, an often unwelcome and unsightly one at that. And the Trickster Scarf taps into that unruly, unplanned, sometimes ugly energy.

This is a project you'll either love or hate. Those witches who are organized, who plan out rituals right down to the word, who color-coordinate their garb, and who keep an indexed and neatly penned Book of Shadows might balk at the hodgepodge way it is put together. Those who are more freeform, who don't know what will happen in their circle until the words leave their mouths, who get lost in the forest and who don't bother with moon phases when they cast a spell might find this project a breath of fresh air. Whichever kind of witch you are (and neither one is better than the other—whatever works for you is valid), I urge you to try this at least once. You may not end up with a scarf you'd want to wear out of the house, but the random energy that will go into the making of it can make it a powerful piece of ritual wear. This scarf can be used in rituals to evoke Trickster gods of various pantheons or where shape-shifting is involved.

This project is one that is best done all in one sitting. It will take about two hours using a sewing machine, longer if you decide to hand stitch it. Before you start, put on some music with a fast, upbeat tempo. Light incense you find invigorating. Gather up your scraps. I like to throw them into a laundry basket, which I set right at my feet as I sit by the sewing machine. That way I can just reach into the basket and pull out a piece of fabric and place it right on the stabilizer as I sew. Keep a pair of scissors on hand to trim the fabric if you need to, but don't spend too much time shaping it. The point is to keep this scarf and the piecing of the scraps as spontaneous as possible. When you are ready, ground and center. Reach out to those parts of you that push against expectations. Get in touch with your inner rebel. Invite the Trickster to come play with you as you sew.

The scraps are sewn onto the stabilizer using long, curving seams. The point is to join the scraps to each other at overlaps. Straight seams won't work here. Use a contrasting thread so that it stands out. Toss in small pieces of ribbon and yarn, bits of lace, and any other sewable scrap that's been hanging out in a shoebox all these years. Keep adding scraps and layering until you feel you've built up a new, rowdy piece of fabric.

1. Cut the water-soluble film stabilizer in half lengthwise.

2. Begin layering fabric scraps at the top edge of a piece of the stabilizer. Sewing from the right to the left, sew the scraps onto the stabilizer. Use long, curving seams.

3. When you have reached the left side, sew back to the right, again using long, curving seams. Space your lines of sewing an inch or two apart, covering as much material as possible.

4. Continue adding scraps and sewing from right to left down the length of the stabilizer.

5. Once you have filled the stabilizer, sew from the top to the bottom several times. The vertical stitching makes sure that all the scrap pieces are secured. Add more scraps as you sew if you feel moved to do so.

6. When you are finished, wash the scarf per the stabilizer instructions. Line dry the scarf.

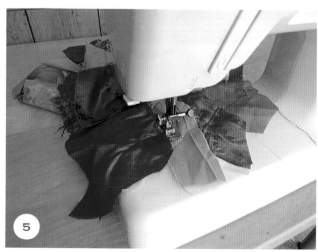

As the scarf grows, it will look like a franken-quilt—that's exactly what you want.

CHARGING

Burn an incense of High John root, mistletoe, juniper, or valerian. Hold the Trickster Scarf over the smoke of the incense. Say,

> *Chameleon, shape-shifter, rapscallion, lend your energies to this scarf, assembled disorganized, chaotic, and disordered.*

Settle the Trickster Scarf over your shoulders, letting the ends hang down in front of you.

> *Powers of illusion, powers to change my form, powers to shift my reality—these all come to me.*

If you are working with a particular Trickster deity, feel free to call on them as you charge the scarf. Afterward, keep it in a safe place, a spell bag or a box, when you are not wearing it.

THIS TECHNIQUE CAN BE USED FOR MORE THAN JUST A SCARF. MAKE SCRAP FABRIC FOR PILLOWS, QUILTS, STUFFED ANIMALS, CLOTHING, AND OTHER PROJECTS THAT COULD USE A TOUCH OF CHAOS.

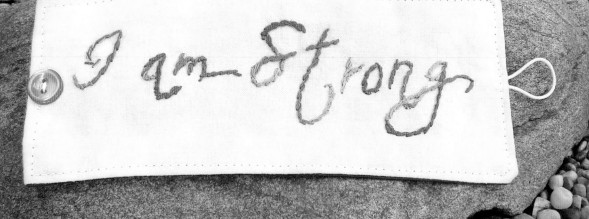

Draw your own affirmation or type it into a word processing program in a font you like. The font used in the pictured cuff is Scriptina. Size the text so it is about 1½" tall and 4" wide, then print it out. Here are a few word suggestions:

Beauty	Healing	Seed
Bountiful	Infinite	Thankful
Calm	Joy	Think
Courage	Open	Transform
Create	Peace	Truth
Dream	Power	Vision
Eternal	Quiet	Wisdom
Gift	Release	
Grow	Respect	

After adding the iron-on interfacing, you can decorate the cuff with beads, studs, buttons, and so on.

This project is suitable for most fabrics. If you choose something that is bulky, you'll need to trim the seams in step 9.

1 Measure your wrist and write down the number. This is your cuff length measurement.

2 Using transfer paper, transfer the affirmation word or phrase onto your fabric using a ballpoint pen.

3 Embroider the word using three strands of floss.

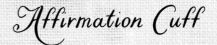
MATERIALS
Transfer paper
12" × 12" piece of fabric
Embroidery thread of a color that stands out against your fabric
Embroidery needle
Medium-weight iron-on interfacing
Thread (any color)
Button
Elastic cord

DIFFICULTY

TIME
2 hours

Affirmations can often get dismissed as "magickal thinking," but this makes them perfect, I think. Wearing a reminder of your magickal intent keeps it at the forefront of your mind. Affirmations seen by others bring intent to their minds as well. This temporary "meeting of the minds" can be used to raise energy for spells. For example, every member of a coven could make a cuff with the affirmation "peace" to wear to a ritual and spellworking for world peace.

This fabric cuff can be also be used by those witches who have to be circumspect about their spellworkings. Embroider your affirmation on the lining instead of the exterior cuff fabric. To everyone else it will look like a piece of jewelry, while you can feel your affirmation next to your skin.

4   Press your fabric from the wrong side to smooth out any wrinkles.

5   Using a ruler, create a rectangle around the affirmation. Make the rectangle as long as your wrist measurement, with the affirmation centered in it. Give the affirmation a 1" margin along the top and bottom to ensure it won't be cut off when you add the lining.

6   Cut out a rectangle of the same width and length from the iron-on interfacing and fabric for a lining. Attach the interfacing to the cuff.

7   Cut out a 1½" length of elastic cording. Bring the ends together to form a loop. Center the loop on one short side of the embroidered cuff, with the ends in line with the edge of the fabric. Tack the loop in place. Have the loop facing in so that when you turn the cuff, it will stick out the right way.

8   With right sides together, sew a ½" seam around the cuff. Start at one long edge, sew around the short end with the loop, and finish at the end of the other long edge. Backstitch at the loop to secure it.

9   Trim the corners. Turn the cuff right-side out. Press.

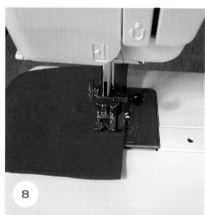

10   Turn the open edge of the cuff in by ½". Press.

11   Topstitch around the cuff to enforce the loop.

12   Attach the button on the other short end of the cuff.

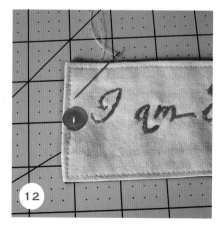

MEASUREMENTS AND MATH

A Measure from the nape of your neck to where you want the robe to fall. Add 1" to this measurement for the hem and then multiply the total by 2. This is your A measurement.

B Measure the length of your outstretched arms from wrist to wrist. Add 2" to that length for the sleeve hems. Divide this total by 2. This is your B measurement.

C Measure loosely around your neck. Divide this measurement by 6. This is your C measurement.

D Measure around your bicep. Add 4" to this measurement for the ease (meaning the looseness of the garment for "ease of movement"). Divide this total by 2. This is your D measurement.

E Measure around your chest. Add 4" to this measurement for the ease. Divide this total by 4. This is your E measurement.

It is a truth universally acknowledged that a Pagan celebrating a sabbat must be in want of a robe. Well, perhaps not so much a "truth." Rituals and spellwork don't require any special attire. I don't throw on a robe every time I work a simple candle spell or draw a rune. But having a special set of clothing for particular events can help put you in the proper frame of mind and lend greater energy to your work.

Cotton is a good choice for robes because it is easy to work with, comfortable, and washable. Satin is a nice choice for a fancier robe. Fabrics like dupioni silk and linen have a texture woven into the fabric that gives it depth. Pick something that feels good against your skin and that is of a light or medium weight. You can use heavy-weight fabrics, but they will be stiff in the way they move and don't drape as well. Solid colors work best and give you the most versatility. Another thing to keep in mind when choosing a fabric is care instructions. Do you want a robe you can toss into the wash, or are you okay with running it to the dry cleaner?

You can decorate your robe in a myriad of ways once you've completed it. Trim can be added to the sleeves, hem, and neckline. Embroidery can also be done, especially at the front neck opening.

With the directions above you can draft a pattern for a robe fitted to your own measurements. Don't let the idea of pattern drafting or math scare you. All the math is simple and making the pattern only involves straight lines. In fact, you will be drawing those lines directly on the fabric. You'll need something to mark the fabric—a pen, pencil, or piece of chalk. Make sure your choice will show up on the fabric. When you are marking out the lines, use a yardstick as a guide so that they are straight and even.

Ritual Robe

MATERIALS
Fabric of any color in the length of your A measurement: If the A measurement is longer than 44", buy 60" wide fabric. If the measurement is longer than 58", you will have to add to the sleeves. See step 9 for further instructions.
Chalk, pen, or pencil for marking
Yardstick
Matching thread
Matching bias binding

DIFFICULTY
✂ ✂ ✂

TIME
2 hours

INSTRUCTIONS

1 Wash, dry, and press your fabric.

2 Fold fabric by first folding it in half lengthwise, right sides together. Then fold the fabric in half widthwise. The folded fabric should be four layers thick.

3 From the folded corner, measure the length of your B measurement along the top fold. Draw a line down from that point the length of your D measurement. This line marks your sleeve length and opening.

4 From the folded corner, measure down your D measurement and then in your E measurement and make a mark. Draw a line from this mark to the line in step 3. This line marks the under seam of your sleeve.

5 Draw a line from the mark in step 4 to the bottom right-hand corner of the fabric. This width will give the robe a dramatic sweep, or you can make it narrower for a more form-fitting silhouette.

6 Draw a curving line in the corner made by the lines in steps 4 and 5. This will give you better ease of movement at the underarm and a more comfortable fit.

7 At the folded corner mark the C measurement along the top and down the side of the fabric. Connect the two marks with a curving line to form the neck opening. The neck opening will be too small at this point. That's okay—you'll be opening it up in the following steps.

8 Cut along the lines through all thicknesses of the fabric.

9 If you need to add to the sleeves, follow these instructions:

A Cut 2 rectangles of matching fabric that measure your bicep measurement plus 4" by the remaining length of fabric you need for your B measurement. To find the remaining length you need to subtract the width of your fabric from your wrist-to-wrist measurement and add the seam allowance. For example if your wrist-to-wrist measurement is 65", your B measurement is 65" plus 2", or 67". If you are using 58" wide fabric, you will need an extra 9" of fabric for full-length sleeves (67 – 58 = 9). In this instance dividing 9" by 2 will tell you that you need to add 4½" to each sleeve. Add 1" to that measurement for the seam allowance.

B Open up the robe and sew the rectangles to each sleeve, right sides of the fabric together, with a ½" seam. Press the seam open to reduce any annoying bulk.

C If you wish to hide the seam on the outside of the robe, add ribbon or other trim over the seam on the right side of the seam.

D Refold the robe at the shoulders, right sides together, and continue as follows.

10 Open the robe along the lengthwise fold. Sew the side seams using a ½" seam allowance from the sleeve opening to the hem on each side. To strengthen the underarm curve, sew again ⅛" from the first stitching inside the seam allowance. Points that see a lot of movement, such as underarm curves, benefit from a second row of stitching as reinforcement.

All manner of inconvenient seams can be covered by the application of a great trim.

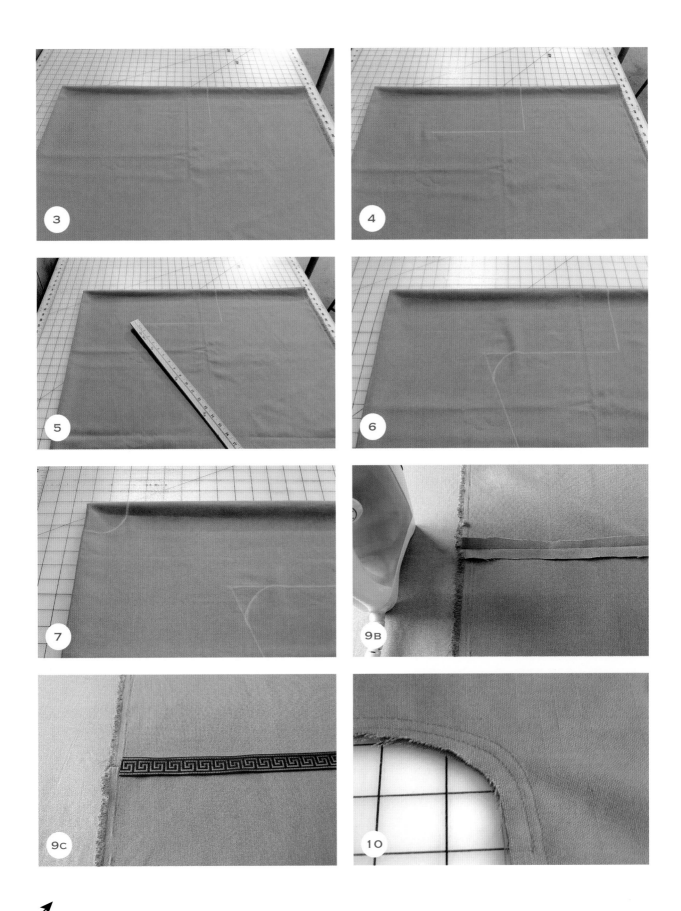

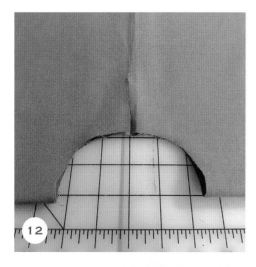

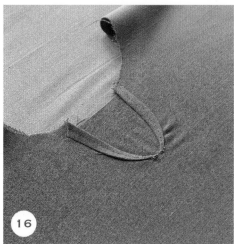

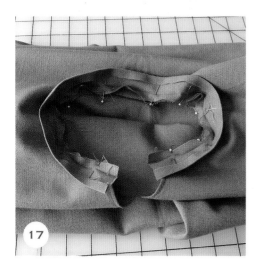

11   Clip the underarm curves.

12   For the neck opening, make a 2-to-3" cut at the center front. Try on the robe. If the neck opening isn't large enough, cut another inch into the slash. Repeat, fitting the robe and adjusting the neck opening until it fits. Start with small slashes. You can always cut open the slash more, but if you cut it open too much, you'll have to stitch the excess closed.

13   Press the side seams open.

14   Hem the sleeve openings with a standard hem.

15   Hem the bottom of the robe with a standard hem.

16   Make a narrow hem of the neck opening slash by sewing ¼" from the edges. Pivot at the bottom of the slash and sew up the other side. Fold the unfinished edges in to the wrong side along the stitching. Press. Fold again and press. This will keep it from unfolding while you sew it in place. Top sew on the outside next to the folded edge around the slash.

17   Finish the neck opening with bias binding. Cut a piece of bias binding 1" longer than the opening. Starting at one of the slash edges, with right sides together, pin the bias binding to the neck opening. Have the bias binding extend ½" beyond the neck opening at each end of the center front. The bias binding will curve with the neck opening.

18   Sew a ¼" seam along the neck opening. Clip curves. Fold extended edges of the bias binding over to the inside of the robe. Fold the bias binding to the wrong side along the seam. Press. Topstitch around the neck opening, backstitching at the beginning and end to secure the edges.

19   Add trim and decoration as desired.

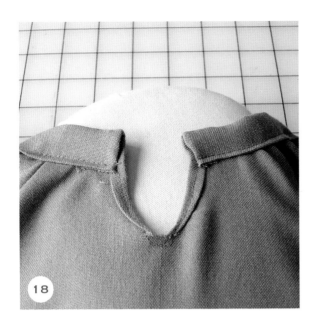

18

Folding the bias binding around the neck opening will cover the unfinished edges and keep them from unraveling.

Hooded Cape

MATERIALS

Fabric of any color in the length of double your A measurement plus your B measurement. If your B measurement is greater than 16", use 60" wide fabric. If it is less than 16", you can use 44" wide fabric.

Lining of any color in the same length as your fabric (if making a lined cape)

Chalk, pen, or pencil for marking

Yardstick

Matching thread

Matching bias binding

Clasp for the closure

DIFFICULTY

TIME

3 hours

MEASUREMENTS AND MATH

A Measure from the nape of your neck to where you want the cape to fall. Add 1" to this measurement for the hem. This is your A measurement.

B Measure loosely around your neck. This is your B measurement.

C Add 6" (for the ease) to your B measurement. This is your C measurement.

D Take your C measurement and multiply it by 3 (for the gathers). Take the resulting number, add 3" (for the seam allowances), and then divide it by 4. This will be your D measurement.

There is something magickal about a cape. Donning one sets the witch apart. It marks them as otherworldly. A cape can add dramatic energy to your spellwork. Plus it is just plain fun to swish around in.

Nearly any fabric can be used for this cape. Before picking out a fabric, consider where you will be wearing your cape, the kind of weather you'll be wearing it in, and so on. For capes that will be worn indoors or in warmer climates, choose lightweight fabrics like silks, cottons, or gauzes. For capes that will be worn outdoors or in colder climates, consider heavier fabrics like wool, suitings, or even fleece. The cape has a gathered neckline and hood, which can result in a bulky seam. If you choose a heavyweight fabric, use a silk or other heavy-duty thread and needle for that seam.

Your cape can be decorated however you wish. Faux fur trim can be added to the hood, or decorative trim can be added along front opening edges. Embroidery can also be used, especially around the clasp. Clasps come in a range of designs and materials. Choose one that will be suitable for the cape fabric (e.g., no heavy metal clasps for a cape made from gauze).

As with the robe pattern, this cape only requires some measurements and a yardstick. You can draw the pattern out on paper beforehand or draw the lines out directly on the fabric. The instructions here include an option to line the cape.

DRAWING A LINE DOWN TO THE LOWER CORNER OF YOUR FABRIC IN STEP 3 WILL GIVE YOU A VERY FULL HEM SUITABLE FOR DRAMATIC SWISHING.

1   Wash, dry, and press your fabric.

2   Lay out the fabric. Cut a length of fabric equal to your B measurement and set aside for the hood. Then cut the remaining fabric into 2 pieces each the length of your A measurement. Fold each piece in half selvage to selvage, right sides together. Lay one length out with the fold facing you. Lay the other length on top of the first with the selvages facing you. This will mean that when you cut out your fabric, you will have 2 front panels and 1 back panel.

3   From the side facing you, measure along the fabric to your D measurement. Mark this point. Using a yardstick, draw a line from your D measurement to the left corner of the fabric. For the hood, fold the fabric you set aside in half, widthwise. Measure the length of your B measurement out from the fold along the top of the fabric. Draw a line from the B measurement down the length of the fabric, making a square.

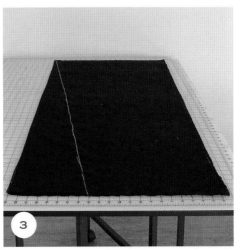

4   Cut along the lines you drew in step 3.

5   With right sides together, sew one front panel to the back panel using a ½" seam. Repeat for the other front panel. This makes the cape body.

6   Press seams open.

7   Mark a spot 1" from the center front opening on both right and left sides along the top edge. This is where you will start and end your gathering stitches. The 1" ungathered fabric will be folded later as part of the front opening hem.

8   Baste ½" from cape top edge between the 2 marks in step 7.

9   Fold the hood fabric in half to make a square.
     Sew a ½" seam on one side of the hood from
     the fold to the edge opposite. This is your cen-
     ter back seam. Press the seam open.

10   On the hood bottom edge (where the center
     back seam is) mark 1" from the end of both
     sides. This is where you will start and end
     your gathering stitches.

11   Baste ½" along hood bottom edge between the
     markings.

12   Gather the hood bottom edge and cape neck
     edge to the length of your C measurement.
     Knot the threads at every end to keep the
     gathers from coming undone. The gathered
     side of your hood should be the same length
     as the gathered neck of the cape.

13   Pin the hood to the cape, right sides together,
     matching center backs and edges. Sew a ½"
     seam. Sew again ⅛" from the first stitching
     inside the seam allowance. Trim the seams.
     *If you are making a lined cape, skip to step 17.
     Otherwise, continue as follows.*

14   To finish the neck seam, cut a piece of bias
     binding 1" shorter than your C measurement.
     Encase the seam in the bias binding, arrang-
     ing it so that there is ½" left exposed on each
     end of the seam. Sew through all thicknesses,
     close to the edges of the bias binding, using
     pins liberally. Press seam down toward cape
     body.

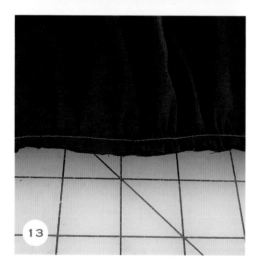

15   Turn under the unfinished edges of the cape
     front and the hood ½" to the wrong side.
     Press. Turn again ½" and press. Make sure to
     cover the unfinished edges of the bias bind-
     ing on the neck seam. Topstitch all along the
     pressed edge close to the first fold.

16 Hem the cape with a standard hem. Continue to step 18.

17 *If making a lined cape:* Make the lining for the cape and hood just as you did for the outer fabric, following steps 1–13. With right sides together, pin the lining to the outer fabric, matching hood centers, neck seams, and hem corners. Sew a ½" seam around all unfinished edges, leaving a 3" wide gap for turning. Turn the cape right-side out through the gap and press the edges. Topstitch around all edges of the cape.

18 Add trim and decoration as desired.

19 Attach the clasp at the neck of the cape.

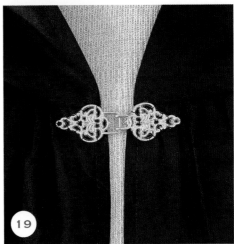

A fancy clasp will make a plain cloak feel more magickal.

The Magickal Home

From hanging horseshoes above the door to catch luck, to offerings made to genius loci when houses were erected, to the worship of domestic deities, much of historical magick is concerned with the home. It's no wonder. Home is where we are supposed to be safe, protected by the walls from the dangers of the world outside. Today, with the economic uncertainty and racial injustice that is so prevalent, a sense of well-being and comfort are more important than ever.

The projects in this section are concerned both with securing one's home and making it a place of comfort, love, peace, and rest. Whether it is a house, apartment, motel room, or other, there are ways to magickally enhance where you hang your hat.

Protective Door Charms

MATERIALS

6" × 6" piece of fabric

Transfer paper

For the sun design: Red, yellow, orange, or gold thread, or a combination of those colors

For the Goddess design: Brown, green, yellow, or gold thread, or a combination of those colors

For the eye design: Blue, green, black, or silver thread, or a combination of those colors

Embroidery needle

Embroidery hoop

DIFFICULTY

✂ ✂ ✂

TIME

30 minutes

Doorways have always been considered magickally charged places. They are necessary to allow us passage into and out of our homes, but that also means unwelcome entities and energies can also enter. As such, there is a host of practices across various cultures and religious beliefs meant to secure doors. A common procedure involves hanging a charm over or next to a door (for example, read about the Abracadabra Charm in the cross stitch section on page 149).

This project offers three designs to choose from for your protective charm. However, if you are still in the broom closet or just looking for other protective sign options, feel free to use symbols from elsewhere. Flowers such as carnations, foxglove, and roses all have protective properties, as do trees such as birch, oak, and willow. Cats, snakes, and ravens all have long-standing associations with witches and can be used as well. If you have a spirit helper, you could embroider a representation of it. Most simply, you can use the word protect. The point is to use a symbol that invokes a sense of protection for you.

This is an excellent project to hone your visualization skills. As you embroider, work mindfully, contemplating what protection means to you. What do you want to feel when you pass the charm on your way out into the world? What do you want to feel when you return? Envision how when you leave, the charm will place a protective cloak on you, one that repels negativity, bad luck, harmful energies, injury, and loss. See how when you return, that same protection extends to keeping those same baleful energies out of your home.

After you make the charms, use the Protection Oil on page 147 to anoint them and amplify the protective energies.

SUN

Along with the eye, the sun is one of the most common and ancient protective symbols. Make this charm and hang it over the door entering your home. When you leave, you'll walk under its protective energies, taking some with you as you go about your business. When you return and enter, the protective rays of the sun will strip away any negativity that might cling to you and try to follow you into your home.

GODDESS

The soft, round image of the Goddess is ancient and carries a deep sense of comfort and safety. Make this charm to bring protection with a maternal aspect. Hang the charm next to your door so that whenever you leave, you feel the protection settle over you like a hug. When you come back, the Goddess's loving safekeeping blocks the entrance to any harm that might try to sneak in with you.

EYE

The eye is a potent source of both protective and harmful magick. The evil eye can be cast, sometimes unconsciously, due to a jealous or covetous gaze. Those suffering from the curse fall victim to bad luck and injury. Talismans to protect against the evil eye take form as eyes also, bringing to mind the saying "an eye for an eye." In ancient Egypt the Eye of Horus and Eye of Ra were both used as protective symbols against misfortune. Hanging an eye next to your door means its unblinking gaze will shine on you when you leave your home, providing you with protection as long as you are out.

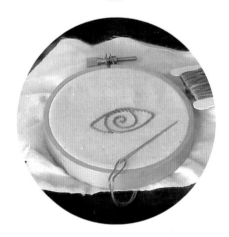

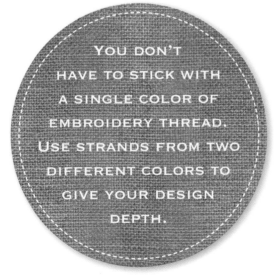

YOU DON'T HAVE TO STICK WITH A SINGLE COLOR OF EMBROIDERY THREAD. USE STRANDS FROM TWO DIFFERENT COLORS TO GIVE YOUR DESIGN DEPTH.

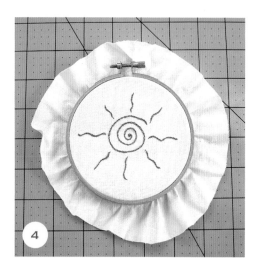

EMBROIDERY INSTRUCTIONS

1 Using tracing paper, trace the desired design from page 234.

2 Using transfer paper, mark the fabric with the design.

3 Center the design in the embroidery hoop. Embroidery hoops hold the fabric taut while you are stitching, ensuring the design doesn't turn out wonky.

4 Embroider the design with 2 strands of embroidery thread. Use a chain stitch for added protective energy, as the chain resembles an eye.

5 When you are finished with the design, iron it using a press cloth.

CHARGING

Anoint your finished charm with the Protection Oil in the sidebar or with your own blend. Run your finger around the outside of the frame or hoop. As you do so, say,

I charge you, charm, to protect me at home and away.
Protect me from injury.
Protect me from illness.
Protect me from negativity.
Protect me from psychic harm.
Protect me from any who wish ill on me.
This is my will, so mote it be.

If you have specific concerns or fears, you can add those to the chant.

Hang the charm either above your door or next to it at eye level. When you leave your home, touch the charm, give it thanks, and know that it is protecting you. When you return, touch it and give thanks again. Keep the charm dusted and recharge it occasionally.

PROTECTION OIL

To 10 milliliters of a carrier oil,
add the following essential oils:

3 drops of rosemary
2 drops of lavender
1 drop of mugwort

Cross Stitch Projects

MATERIALS

Embroidery thread as per charts on
    pages 235–38
18" × 8" 14-point Aida cloth

DIFFICULTY

✂ ✂ ✂

TIME

1–2 hours

The first embroidery projects I was introduced to were counted cross stitch. I loved the bright colors of the floss, the simplicity of the two stitches, and the rigidity of the Aida cloth. Within those limitations, a universe of magick could be made, much like ritual magick.

Over the years there has been an explosion of cross stitch designs. Country cottages and Pennsylvania Dutch samplers now rub elbows with snarky quotes and science fiction portraits. A new generation of stitchers has found expression in a traditional medium, and it is delightful.

The following designs can be stitched in an evening. They can be framed, turned into pillows, put on bags, or used as patches. Work the cross stitch with two strands and the back stitch with one strand. The colors in the chart are recommendations and can be substituted with hues of your choice.

These samplers can also be stitched as a form of dynamic meditation, like creating sand paintings or coloring mandalas. The repetition of the borders is soothing, and they lend themselves to meditative action. Coordinate the colors to the mood or concern you are meditating on to deepen the exercise.

WICCAN REDE SAMPLER

The Wiccan Rede has a tangled and confusing history; however, it has been adopted by many Wiccans and Pagans the world over. Whatever the origin, it has a sentiment that corresponds nicely with my own world-view. Also, it is a recognizable sentiment that marks out one's religious beliefs, much like a crucifix or pentagram. I purposely surrounded the phrase with flowers and a spiralesque border to amplify the sentiment behind the words.

The flowers also echo the sweetness of more traditional samplers while the spiral in the upper left corner is a direct reference to the spiral, a symbol of life, death, rebirth, and the Goddess.

DO NO HARM BUT TAKE NO SHIT

In contrast to the Wiccan Rede, "Do no harm but take no shit" is a relatively new phrase in the Pagan lexicon. There is a belief, at times, that pacifism, kindness, and so on are signs of weakness. However, I believe that people who go out of their way to bring light to the world aren't doormats to be stepped on by more aggressive, "pragmatic" people.

The design was created with a Greek shield in mind. It's an allusion to shielding yourself from any negativity as you go about the business of being the good in the world.

MAIDEN, MOTHER, CRONE

The Triple Goddess is a foundational belief in many Pagan paths. It can be hard to relate to the aspects of the Goddess that you haven't yet experienced. Especially in Western society, we give lip service to the wisdom of elders but worship youth over all. We have a conflicted and contentious relationship with mothers, simultaneously putting them on a pedestal and tearing them down. We fete and cater to youth but dismiss the concerns of young people.

This design is meant to take the celebration of all the aspects of the Goddess and put them front and center. We can all dance, we can all laugh, we can all think. These are aspects of the Goddess we can incorporate in our lives and that can allow us to get in touch with her three phases.

ABRACADABRA CHARM

The first recorded use of the word charm *abracadabra* was by Quintus Serenus Sammonicus, a Roman physician in the third century CE in his book *Liber medicinalis*. He writes (as translated by Chris Francese):

> The malady the Greeks call hemitritaeos is more deadly. None of our ancestors could name this disease in our own language, nor did they feel the need to. On a piece of parchment, write the so-called "abracadabra" several times, repeating it on the line below; but take off the end, so that gradually individual letters, which you will take away each time, are missing from the word. Continue until the (last) letter makes the apex of a cone. Remember to wind this with linen and hang it around the neck. Many people say that the lard of a lion is effective . . .

While his version was written and then hung around the neck as an amulet against *hemitritaeos* (a fever that caused seizures), this project creates a similar charm to hang near your doorway or to carry in your bag to head off illness. The cross stitch pattern is sewn with two threads of black floss. You could substitute the black for blue or other colors associated with healing.

While stitching the design, visualize healing energies flowing from your hands and heart into the fabric and thread. Call upon healing deities and spirits to aid you in the work. If you are creating a charm for someone who is ill, picture the illness fading away, just as the letters of the word disappear in each successive line.

Hang it near the doorway of your home or near the sick person. If used for a person who is ill, once the illness has abated, roll up the charm, tie with a length of red cord, and bury or burn it. If the charm is hung as a preventative and you no longer want it hanging around, roll it up, binding with a length of red cord, and store it away until you have need of it once more.

You can also carry the charm with you, again rolled up and tied with a red cord.

While the word *abracadabra* is the most familiar "disappearing" talisman used, it is not the only one. In his book *Trolldom,* Johannes Björn Gårdbäck notes that the word *Almagata* is used in the same manner for the cold or flu. Each letter at the end is dropped on each successive line until only "alm" is left. This opens up possibilities of creating one's own illness talisman.

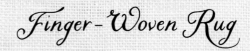

Finger-Woven Rug

Finger weaving is one of the simplest weaving techniques. All it requires is your hands and material. I first learned how to finger weave in school. I went through a phase where no stray yarn was safe around me, and I managed to make yards of finger-woven cords. These mostly went to making hair bands for my various dolls.

A couple of decades later I found myself with several fleece scarves at the end of my convention season. I knew I wasn't going to make any more, and the ones I had on hand hadn't sold since I had made them two years before. Not wanting to waste perfectly good fabric, I cut them apart into 1" wide strips and pieced them together. Then, dusting off a technique I hadn't used in what felt like forever, I started weaving. When I had used up all the fleece, I had a long, snake-like pile of cord piled at my feet.

An hour more with a plastic canvas needle, yarn, and some non-slip rug backing, I had my first rug. It now lies on the floor beside my bed. Before I go to sleep at night and when I get up in the morning, my feet land on it. The colors of camel, dark green, and sage green are soothing to me, and the spiral catches my attention, giving me a few seconds of calm before I go about the business of sleep or facing the day. The fleece is soft and warm, which is a bonus on cold winter mornings.

Another rug stands inside the entrance of my workshop. Whenever I step into it, I am reminded that I am entering sacred space, and when I leave, the rug's blue, black, and gray spirals remind me that I am leaving that space.

Make one of these rugs to serve as such a spot check. Or make one to serve as a meditation mat. Or empower the spiral to trap negative energy before it can enter your home. However you decide to use the rug, choose fabric colors that match your intentions. Use shades of blue, purple, and silver, for example, for a meditation mat. Or choose colors that you find empowering for a bedside rug. (See the color correspondences on page 219 for suggestions.)

MATERIALS
2 yards of fleece
Yarn in a coordinating color
Plastic canvas needle
Non-slip rug backing

DIFFICULTY

TIME
2 hours

SHOULD THE RUG GET SOILED, SIMPLY UNDO ITS STITCHING, WASH THE FLEECE COIL, AND THEN REASSEMBLE IT WHEN IT HAS DRIED. IF YOU ARE USING THE RUG AS A NEGATIVITY TRAP, REGULARLY CLEANSE IT WITH A FULL MOON BATH.

1 Cut the fleece in 1" wide strips.

2 Make a small snip at each end of the strips.

3   Thread one strip (A) through the hole of another strip (B). Then bring the free end of strip A through the hole of its own far end. Pull strip A through its hole until it tightens as a knot around strip B. These two connected strips are now your strip B. In essence you are creating a loop of strip A through the hold at the end of strip B.

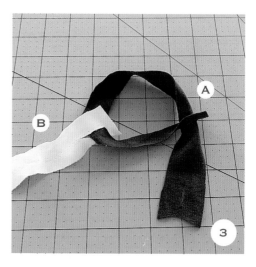

4   Repeat step 3 with a new strip A until you have one long strip of fleece.

5   Loop the snipped hole at the end of the fleece strip over the thumb of your non-dominant hand.

6   Starting at the front of your index finger, wrap the fleece around the back of your middle finger and bring it back around your index finger, creating a figure eight. Keep the fleece loose.

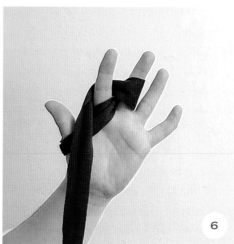

7   Now pull the bottom loop of fleece over the top of the loose fleece and over your index finger. This will make a loop around your index finger. You should have one strip of fleece in front of your index finger and two behind it.

8   Bring the free end of the fleece in front of your middle finger, and again pull the bottom loop of fleece over this top loose fleece and over your middle finger, creating a loop. You are repeating the motion in step 7 with your middle finger.

9   Bring the free end of the fleece around the back of both your middle finger and index finger, and then around to the front of your index finger.

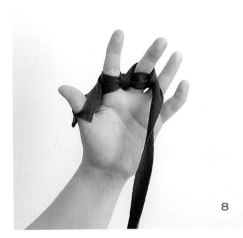

8

9

10

10 Repeat steps 6–8 until you have used up all the fleece. Once you've made several passes, you can remove the fleece loop from your thumb and let it hang down the back of your hand. Occasionally, give the end of the coil a gentle tug to expand it.

11 When you have finished, tie a knot at both ends of the fleece coil.

12 Roll the fleece coil into a spiral. (Photo on next page.)

13 As you roll, use yarn and a plastic canvas needle to sew the coil together through the gaps in the weave. Push the needle through the weave and stitch the coil to its neighbor. (Photo on next page.)

14 Once you have finished the spiral, cut out a piece of non-slip rug backing to the size of the rug.

15 Use more yarn and your plastic needle to sew the rug onto the backing. Sew around the outside and make a cross stitch at the center to secure the backing to the rug. (Photo on next page.)

Charge your rug with visualization and essential oils, if you wish.

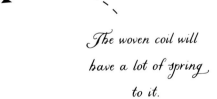

The woven coil will have a lot of spring to it.

12

13

15

ALTERNATE USE

The spiral form of this rug can also be used protectively. Sew as instructed, but when sewing, visualize all negativity wandering the spiral and becoming trapped at the center. Say,

Wander, wander, negativity—
Lost, never to be found.

Place the rug at your front door so that you step on it when you first come home. Any clinging negative energy will be trapped by the rug.

Once a month lay it out under the waning moon to get rid of any trapped negativity.

In my backyard I have a bower on which morning glories entwine. I have always loved the cheerful face the flowers give to the day, especially as I am not a morning person. I can see the blooms from my bedroom window, and so no matter how grouchy I might be when I drag myself from the warm embrace of my bed, I smile when I catch sight of the blue and purple flowers.

Morning glory seeds added to dream pillows keep nightmares at bay. Perhaps this is because they carry in them a promise of the morning to come, when the sunrise banishes the monsters of the night.

Make dream pillows to help with prophetic dreams or to ease your mind to sleep. Make one for the child who wakes up from nightmares. She can reach for her sleep pillow, inhale the scent of lavender and lemon balm, and fall back asleep, knowing her dreams will be sweetened by the scents. Look to the list of sleep and dream deities in the appendix for aid in choosing a deity to invoke in your work if you wish.

Dream Pillow

MATERIALS

2 pieces of blue fabric, one 8" × 8"
    and one 5" × 5"
Transfer paper
5" × 5" piece of lightweight fusible
    interfacing
Embroidery thread in blue, purple,
    and silver
Embroidery hoop and needle
Thread
9 morning glory seeds
¼ cup dried lavender

DIFFICULTY

TIME

2 hours

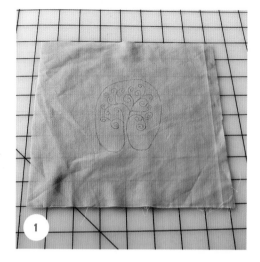

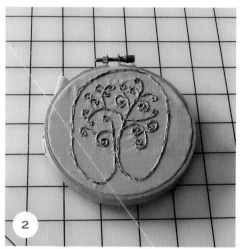

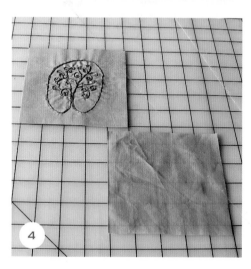

Various cultures have their own symbols of sleep. Below are a few examples:

Japanese: Baku is a supernatural being that devours bad dreams. If woken up from a nightmare, a child can call out, "Baku-san, come eat my dream!"

Yoruban: Olokun, coral

Ojibwe: Asibikaashi, dreamcatcher

Greek: Hypnos, Morpheus, poppies

Irish: Caer Ibormeith, swans

Some crystals are considered helpful for sleep. Amethyst helps with insomnia and nightmares, while peridot protects against bad dreams. You can either use them in charging the pillow or include small bits of crystal in with the stuffing. Additionally, the color blue is associated with prophetic dreams and protection during sleep, while the color silver is associated with dreams. Both colors can be included in your fabric and embroidery thread choices to add their energies to the pillow.

For the thread, use silk to inspire your dreams or cotton for deep rest. For the fabric, use linen for its association with the water element.

You can replace the lavender in this craft with another herb for a different effect. Mugwort and marigold can be used instead to encourage prophetic dreams. To stop nightmares, use morning glory seeds, lemon verbana, vervain, anise, wood betony, mullein, purslane, rosemary, or thyme. To ensure peaceful sleep, use mistletoe, rosemary, or thyme. You can use a mix of the herbs as well. Keep the total volume of dried herbs to ¼ cup to fit the pillow.

1 Make a copy of the dreaming tree design on page 239. Using transfer paper, transfer the embroidery design onto the 8" × 8" piece of fabric.

2 Using an embroidery hoop, stitch the design with 3 strands of embroidery thread (1 blue, 1 purple, 1 silver). Use a stem, chain, or split stitch.

3 When finished, apply fusible interfacing to the back of the design.

4 With the design centered, cut the fabric out in a 5" square. Make sure to leave enough room around the design so that it doesn't get cut off by the seam in the next step.

5 With right sides together, stitch a ½" seam along all sides of the square, leaving a 3" gap for turning. Backstitch at the start and finish of the seam.

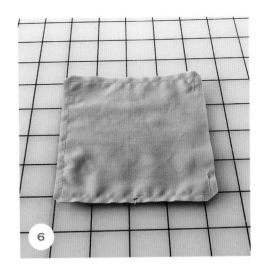

6 Trim the corners and seam allowances. This will ensure that the corners are well defined and not lumpy when you turn the pillow right-side out.

7 Turn the pillow right-side out. Press.

8 Stuff the pillow with 9 morning glory seeds and ¼ cup of dried lavender flowers. Do not overstuff. You can consecrate your herbs and seeds before you stuff the pillow if you wish.

9 Topstitch ⅛" around all sides of the pillow. This not only closes the gap but also adds a nice decorative finishing touch. Work slowly, shifting the lavender and morning glory seeds to the center to avoid catching them in the needle.

CHARGING

Hold the pillow in both hands and charge it with restful sleep intentions. Say,

> Lavender sweet and glory of day,
> Keep any nightmares at bay.
> Should I wake before the dawn,
> Send me back to the land of Nod.

You can call upon one of the gods of sleep or dreams to bless the pillow as well.

Place the dream pillow under your own. Should you awake during sleep, grip your dream pillow, inhale the lavender scent, and allow it to lull you back to sleep.

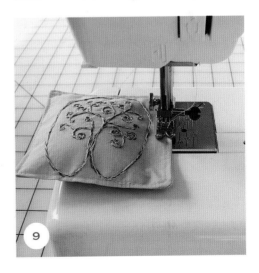

Sleep Mask

MATERIALS

¼ yard exterior fabric
¼ yard lining fabric
¼ yard thin cotton batting
11" length of ¼" elastic (more or less,
 depending on the size of your head;
 see instructions)
Thread

DIFFICULTY

TIME

1 hour

Perhaps, like me, you suffer from insomnia, or maybe you want to boost your chances of having prophetic dreams. Maybe you just want to block out the early morning light that keeps waking you up before your alarm goes off. Now is the time to make an sleep mask for yourself, charged with magickal intent to get you the most out of your slumber.

Choose a soft fabric, at least for the inside of the sleep mask. Flannel is a good choice. Colors such as blue, purple, and black and designs of spirals, stars, and clouds tap into the energy of sleep.

Enhance the effectiveness of your mask by anointing the exterior with lavender or chamomile oil. Do not anoint the inside of the mask, as that can lead to eye irritation.

1 Using a tape measure, find the length from one ear to the other around the back of your head. This is how long you should cut your elastic.

2 Using tracing paper, trace the pattern piece for the sleep mask on page 240. Cut out the pattern.

3 Cut out 1 pattern piece each of the exterior fabric, lining fabric, and cotton batting. The 3 layers of fabric mean that no light will be getting through to disturb your sleep.

4 Tack the elastic to the right side of the exterior fabric at the dots marked on the pattern, inside the seam allowance, to keep it in place.

5 Place the cotton batting on the wrong side of the lining fabric. Baste around all edges.

6 With right sides together, sew the lining and the exterior fabric together using a ¼" seam, leaving the space open between the triangles marked on the pattern. Backstitch over the elastic at both dots to reinforce the hold. Be careful not to catch the elastic in the stitching.

7 Trim the cotton batting inside the seam to reduce bulk.

8 Clip the curves.

9 Turn the mask right-side out. Use a chopstick or other turning tool to smooth the curves.

10 Press the mask.

11 Topstitch around the mask edges, closing the opening.

While working on the sleep mask, keep in mind the purpose you have for it. Need to get more sleep? Envision soft blue light flowing from the fabric as you work. Hear the sounds of slumber in the hum of your sewing machine. Creating a mask to aid you in prophetic dreams? See the color purple infusing the fabric, and see the movement of the needle, in and out, as the waves of water, the element of dreams.

When topstitching, take care not to catch the elastic on the stitching.

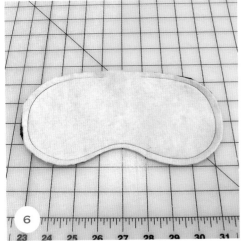

CONSECRATION

When you have finished your mask, consecrate it thus:

Before you retire for the evening place the sleep mask on your altar. Make a cup of chamomile or some other herbal tea that induces sleep. Waft the sleep mask through the fragrant steam of the tea. Say,

> *To sleep fast, sleep to last, sleep to dream, meaning to gleam.*

You can call on a deity associated with sleep and dreams, such as Hypnos or Morpheus, or call on your patron deity for protection while you sleep.

You can recharge your sleep mask occasionally with a moon bath during the full moon.

It's in the Bag

I am a sucker for bags. From tiny organza pouches for wedding favors to backpacks with a million and one compartments, I love them all. The way some witches collect jars for materia magica, I make and collect bags. I feel very keenly that a bag's usefulness cannot be overstated. It is in that frame of mind that I present this collection of bags.

The projects in this section range from the humble pouch to a multipocketed bag for holding runes and crystals. Each is useful in a variety of ways. Whip up some drawstring Rectangular Pouches for the Prosperity Sachets on page 204 or make the Foraging Bag for a weekend hike to gather herbs.

In traditions all over the world, bags are used in ritual and magick. Countless examples of the magickal pouch abound. In her book *Textiles,* Beverly Gordon writes about the Osage in North America, who would create feast bags. "The bags helped build power through their imagery (zigzags represented lightning and the regenerative powers of the metaphoric bison) and their form (their wide rectangular shape alluded to a pregnant bison). The weavers sang ceremonial chants as they made these containers, further infusing them with sacred presence."

Call them gris-gris, hoodoo bags, prayer bundles, or what have you, pouches are more than just bags of holding. They have their own magick energy that can be harnessed to enhance your sewing spellwork. The following are several different pouch types for various skill levels and uses.

Circular Pouch

MATERIALS

1 circular piece of suede, any size
Cording twice the length of the
 circumference of the suede circle
Plastic canvas needle
Awl

DIFFICULTY

TIME

30 minutes

This is as basic as a pouch gets. Take a piece of cloth, cut it in a circle, poke holes around the edge, and lace a cord through the holes, and you have a pouch. As basic as it is, though, it is also versatile. Embroider power symbols in the middle of the circle. Add beads and charms to enhance its magickal purpose. Add trim along the outside to make a fancy wearable amulet.

These pouches work best with leather, suede, felt, wool, and other materials that don't fray when cut. If you are using cotton or other fraying fabrics, you can finish the edges with a narrow hem.

1 If you wish to decorate the pouch, do so now, adding decoration to the right side of the fabric. Otherwise, lay the fabric down with the wrong side of the fabric up. Mark an even number of points at even intervals about ½" in from the edge of the circle.

2 Use the awl to poke holes at the mark.

3 Thread the cording on the plastic canvas needle and thread it through the holes, starting from the right side of the fabric.

4 Knot the cord ends.

Rectangular pouches are multipurpose containers for everything from herbs to tarot cards to sewing supplies. There are endless decoration choices, and they can be made up into sizes to fit practically anything.

1   Fold fabric over with right sides facing each other and sew the two long sides together up from the folded edge to 1" from the top.

2   Fold the short sides of the opening down ½" wrong side to wrong side and sew close to the edge.

3   Cut a length of cord twice the width of the pouch plus 5" (for example, if the pouch is 10" wide, cut 25" of cord). Thread the cording through the channels. Knot the cording.

Rectangular Pouch

MATERIALS

1 rectangular piece of fabric that is as
   wide and twice as long as you need
Thread
Cording

DIFFICULTY

TIME

30 minutes

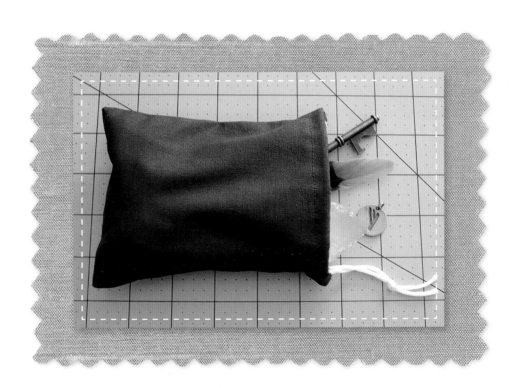

CHOOSE A FABRIC
DESIGN THAT SPEAKS
TO HIKING IN THE
FOREST OR COMBING
THE BEACH.

Foraging Bag

MATERIALS
1 yard outer fabric
1½ yards lining fabric
Thread

DIFFICULTY
✂ ✂ ✂

TIME
2 hours

There is one tool in the witch's inventory that often goes overlooked. Before they can hang herbs to dry, before they can set stones on altars, before they can add ingredients to the cauldron, the witch must gather those components. The witch's bag has long been a source of mystery and curiosity. Into it goes the materia magica of spells and rituals. And just because the bag is a purely functional item doesn't mean it warrants less regard than the other tools the witch uses in their foraging.

The story of the bag that follows is one of necessity. I wanted a collection bag, a simple one. It had to be big enough to hold a good amount of plant and mineral matter, but not so big that I had to rustle around in it to find what I had collected. It had to have interior pockets so that smaller or more delicate items could be kept from getting lost amongst the twigs and roots. And it had to not require any hardware because I didn't want to have to go out and buy anything special to make it.

I spent several months browsing Pinterest and trying out bag patterns I found there. All of them left me disappointed in one way or another. Eventually, I decided to just draft my own pattern. That was the start of another few months of tweaking the design over and over until I was finally happy. The first bag I made was from a length of unbleached linen embroidered with a scattering of white-petaled flowers, with golden centers. Gold thread vines snake around from one cluster of flowers to the next.

Whenever I go out foraging in the small park next to home, my first step is to grab my bag. It is a signal to my witchy brain about the task at hand. This shift in attitude helps me center and leave the house with my intentions firmly in mind.

In fact, I have found this bag so useful that it accompanies me on pathworking. I use an astral bag in its image on those journeys during which I collect items or receive gifts from the spirits I encounter. This sort of connection between the physical and astral amplifies my connection to spirit.

The design here is simple but hardworking. Pick a fabric that is durable for both the exterior and the lining.

BECAUSE IT DOESN'T HAVE ANY HARDWARE, THIS BAG CAN BE MACHINE WASHED, SOMETHING ELSE TO TAKE INTO ACCOUNT WHEN YOU ARE DECIDING ON FABRIC.

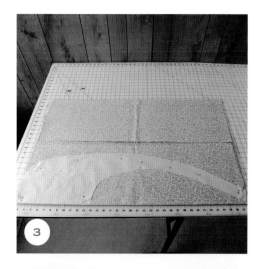

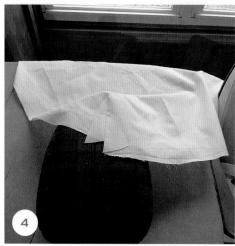

1   Wash, dry, and press the fabric.

2   Using tracing paper, trace the pattern pieces for the bag on pages 241–45. Cut them out and assemble them.

3   Fold the selvages into the center of the fabric so that they meet and form two folds on the outer edge. This way makes the best use of it and reduces waste. Cut out 2 body pieces of the outer fabric and 2 body pieces of the lining fabric. Cut 4 pieces of the pocket from the lining fabric.

4   Sew darts in the body pieces and lining. Mark the darts on the wrong side of the fabric. Cut the center line just short of the point to make sure the fabric is distributed evenly on either side of the center line. Pin the dart together, right sides facing. Sew from the bottom of the dart to the point, backstitching at the beginning. Change your stitch length to the shortest stitch 1" away from the point and finish by sewing directly on the fold at the very end. Press the darts open. Remember to set your stitch length back before you start the next seam.

5   With right sides together, matching the darts, sew the outer fabric body pieces together along the outside with a ½" seam. Press the seam open. Turn the body right-side out and topstitch close to the seam.

6 With right sides facing each other, sew 2 pocket pieces together, with a ½" seam around all edges, leaving a small space along the top edge for turning. Turn the pocket right-side out and press. Topstitch along the top ⅛" from the edge. Repeat for the other set of pocket pieces.

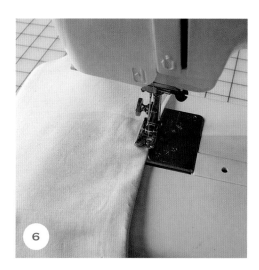

7 Position the pocket onto the lining, matching up dots. Pin. Sew a ¼" seam around the curved sides, backstitching at the start and end of the stitch to reinforce it. Sew a ⅛" seam from the edge of the curved side, again backstitching at the start and stop. Finally, sew a ⅜" seam from the curved edge, backstitching at the start and stop. Repeat with the other pocket on the remaining lining.

8 With right sides together, sew the lining body pieces together along the outside seam. Press the seam open.

9 Matching notches and with right sides together, sew the lining to the outer fabric along the inner edge. Leave the strap ends open for turning. Make sure to backstitch at the beginning and ends of seams.

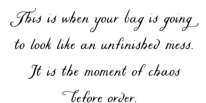

This is when your bag is going to look like an unfinished mess. It is the moment of chaos before order.

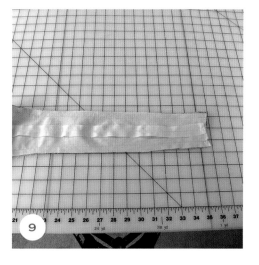

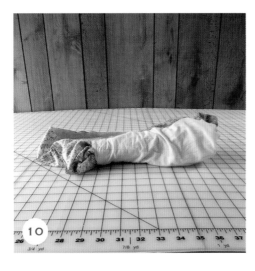

10 Turn the bag right-side out through one of the strap end openings. Work slowly, using a turning tool (or chopstick) to push the bulk of the fabric through the narrow opening. This step looks awkward—don't be daunted.

11 Push the lining into the body of the bag. Press the interior seams. Fold the ends of one strap opening in and press. Insert the other strap opening into the pressed strap end and pin it in place.

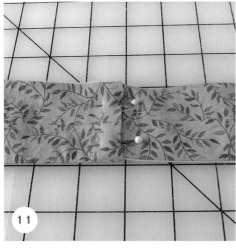

12 Edge stitch along both sides of the bag interior. Stitch a rectangle over the point where the strap ends meet and then stitch a diagonal line from each corner to the opposite corner, making an X.

Use an X box stitch to reinforce the strap overlap.

I have a small collection of tarot decks that I've picked up or have been gifted over the years. I like to use the cards in ritual or to see how a project will turn out. Despite having a small hoard, I favor one deck in particular: *The Herbal Tarot* by Michael Tierra. I used to carry it everywhere with me, but the box was getting battered and bruised from all the jostling. I didn't want to consign my deck to a rubber band, so I made up a tarot sleeve. Not only does it keep my cards together and protected, but the black cloth helps keep unwanted energies from sticking to the deck.

I have other sleeves for attuning my cards to various intentions and energies. Am I going to do a reading for a new project? I slip my cards into the purple sleeve for inspiration. Charging my cards with lunar energy? I place them into the silver sleeve before putting them out under the moonlight.

These sleeves use knit fabric, which stretches, so you can slip objects (crystals, metals, coins, etc.) in with your cards for extra enhancement. They are very easy to make and use very little fabric. You might find yourself making one for each deck in your collection.

Tarot Sleeve

MATERIALS

1 piece of knit fabric measuring your A measurement by your B measurement (the width should go with the stretch of the fabric)

Thread

Ballpoint needle if machine sewing

DIFFICULTY

TIME

1 hour

MEASUREMENTS AND MATH

A Measure the width of the two sides and front of your deck. This is your A measurement.

B Measure your deck's length by wrapping the tape measure around all four sides. Add 1½" to this measurement. This is your B measurement.

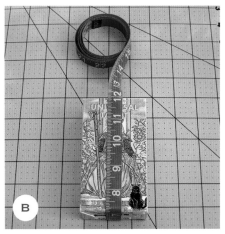

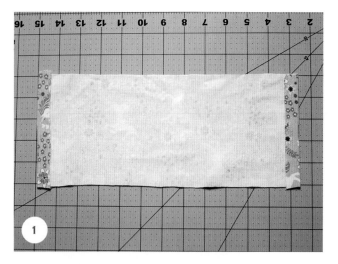

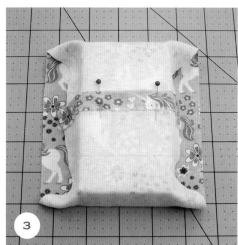

1 Fold each short end of the fabric in ½", wrong side to wrong side. Press.

2 Use a zigzag stitch to close the edge of each fold. These folds will be the finished opening of the sleeve.

3 Wrap the fabric around your deck, wrong side facing out. Line up the seams. Make sure the top flap is underneath the bottom flap; this ensures the finished sleeve opens correctly. Pin the opening and slide the deck out from the fabric.

4 Sew a ½" seam along both long sides using a zigzag stitch. As long as the fabric you use isn't heavy and thick, you don't have to trim the seams.

5 Turn the sleeve right-side out. Use a chopstick to push the corners out.

6 Slip your tarot deck into the sleeve.

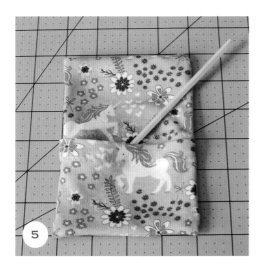

5

REDUCE, REUSE, RECYCLE

You don't have to hit the fabric store every time you start a sewing project. Lots of material can be found easily and cheaply at thrift stores or garage sales—even in the depths of your own closet. Due to the sheer volume of donations, much of the clothing sent to charities every year ends up in landfills. Projects like the Tarot Sleeve are perfect for scavenged fabrics, old T-shirts especially. Repurposing clothing that you already have lying around or scavenging materials from charities helps keep that material out of the garbage heap.

Be gentle when pushing the corners out so as not to poke through the fabric.

Crystal / Rune Storage Bag

MATERIALS

2 rectangles of lining fabric, 9" × 12"

2 squares of lining fabric, 9" × 9"

2 squares of exterior fabric, 9" × 9"

Matching thread

1 circle of exterior fabric with
  a diameter of 4½"

1 circle of heavy-duty double-sided craft
  interfacing with a diameter of 3¼"

1 circle of lining fabric with a diameter
  of 4½"

Chalk, pen, or pencil for marking

2 pieces of ⅞" grosgrain ribbon
  9" in length

1½ yards of satin rattail cording

DIFFICULTY

✂ ✂ ✂

TIME

1 hour

I first designed this bag to hold my various dice, counters, tokens, and minis that I used in roleplaying games like Dungeons & Dragons. In my designing of it I decided that I was going to make a pretty bag, which led me to name the design My Pretty Dice Bag. During the first convention I vended at with the bags, I encountered men coming to my booth saying they heard I had dice bags with pockets on the inside. Upon seeing the bags, the universal question I got was, "Why are they all so girlie?" I proceeded to tell each and every one of those men that it was because I was a horrible sexist who only made gaming supplies for girls. The men would give me looks of confusion, while their wives and girlfriends would cheer and grab a bag for themselves.

Since I first designed it, this bag has been bought and used by others for more than just d20s. It is a really handy bag that lends itself to any number of uses. The pockets allow you to keep things organized, while the flat, reinforced bottom helps the bag stand upright. People have used it to store jewelry, makeup, runes, crystals, lace tatting supplies, handheld game players, and much more.

All sorts of fabric are suitable for the exterior: cottons, taffetas, silks, velvets, and so on. Choose colors and designs that are in line with what you plan for the bag to hold. Lining material is best for the inside, although lightweight cotton can be used in a pinch.

1. Fold the lining rectangle in half lengthwise to create a 9" × 6" rectangle. Press the fold. Fold the rectangle again to create a 4½" × 6" rectangle. Press the fold; this creates a guide for the seam in step 2. Open up the second fold and pin the rectangle to the lining square matching up the bottoms. Repeat with the second lining rectangle.

2. Sew down the middle fold of the pockets, making sure to backstitch at the start.

3. Pin the lining squares and pocket pieces together, pockets facing in, and sew ½" side seams.

4. With right sides facing together, sew ½" side seams on the exterior fabric.

5. Baste along the bottom of the lining piece and the exterior fabric piece ½" from the edge.

6. Prepare the bottom exterior piece by fusing the craft interfacing in the center of the wrong side of the bottom circle. Once fused, there should be ½" of the fabric showing all the way around. (Photo on next page.)

Just sew along the fold and you'll have side interior pockets in the finished bag.

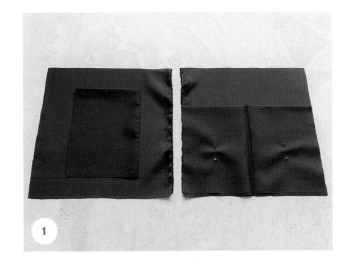

7 Gather up the basting thread on the exterior piece so that it will fit the bottom circle. Once you have the size right, tie the gather threads together to prevent slipping and then pin the two pieces together. Sew the bottom to the exterior piece.

8 Repeat with the lining piece and the bottom lining circle. Note: the bottom lining circle will *not* have craft interfacing.

9 Turn the lining piece right-side out and place it inside the exterior piece, matching side seams.

10 Sew the lining piece to the exterior piece with a ½" seam. Leave an opening of about 3" for turning the bag.

11 Turn the back right-side out through the opening. Voilà! No unfinished seams to be seen.

12 Push the lining down into the exterior. Press the top edge with an iron. Keeping the fabric taut to prevent bunching, topstitch the folded edge. This will close the opening you used to turn the bag and give it a nice clean finish.

13 Mark a line 1" from the top edge with chalk or a marking pencil. Place the top edges of the grosgrain ribbons along this line, making sure the ends overlap the side seams of the bag.

14 Topstitch close to the top and bottom edge of the ribbons, folding under the overlap on each side so that the ribbons butt up against each other but do not overlap.

15 Thread the drawstring through the channel. Cut the 1½ yards of rattail cording in half (so that you have 2 pieces that are 27" long). Using a drawstring tool or large safety pin, thread 1 piece of cording through the channel, exiting at the starting point. Then thread the remaining cording starting at the opposite opening. Threading the cording in this way allows you to close the finished bag by pulling on both cord ends.

16 Tie the ends of the drawstrings.

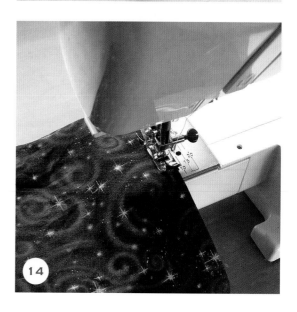

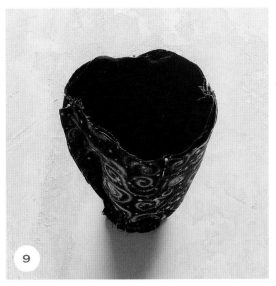

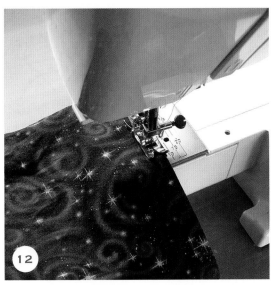

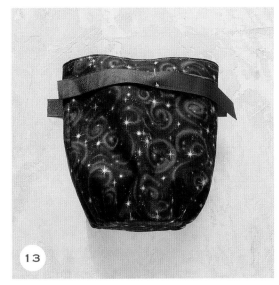

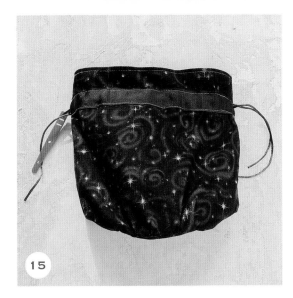

The ends of the ribbons will be folded over, which is why the pieces have to be cut longer than the width of the opening.

*This easy project can also keep
your lip balm close at hand and
out of the wash.*

Modern Enchantment

These days we are so dependent on electronics. Work and leisure often involve computers. Our social lives are lived via apps on our phones. While some might rail against this brave new world, I find it exciting. With so much entrusted to our gadgets, we need modern magick to protect it all.

There are several gods and goddesses the modern witch can work with for help with their electronics. Mercury, Freya, Papa Legba, and Iris all are associated with communication. They can be called on to ensure your emails and texts relay exactly what you mean or to give your words an extra boost when you are trying to persuade someone. Tir, Seshat, Oghma, and Nidaba all are deities of writing. Invoke them to keep your messages free from typos and misspellings.

Any of the above deities can be invited to lend their energy to the two following projects: a soft Phone Case and a keychain USB Holder.

Phone Case

MATERIALS

2 rectangular pieces of craft-weight double-sided fusible interfacing that are ½" wider than your A measurement and your B measurement

2 rectangular pieces of fabric that are 1½" wider than your A measurement and twice as long as your B measurement plus 1"

Binder clip

Thread

DIFFICULTY

TIME

1 hour

MEASUREMENTS AND MATH

A Measure your phone from one side to the other. This is your A measurement.

B Measure your phone from the top to the bottom. This is your B measurement.

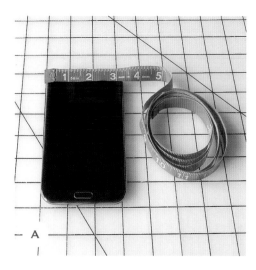

Over the past several years, a field of techno-magick has emerged. Using the ubiquitous cell phone, witches are using text, email, and even emojis to work spells. All you need is an intention and a connection and you can work your magick over the radio waves.

With such a powerful talisman in your pocket, it makes sense to give it a layer of magickal protection along with a passcode. The project below makes a soft case that can be marked with any number of protective symbols. You could even use the same fabric for a matching USB holder (page 180) to coordinate protection of all your data.

Use silver or yellow fabric to tap into the colors' communication properties. Most fabrics are suitable for this project; however, avoid fabric with glitter, sequins, or other embellishments that might scratch the screen. Make sure to use a press cloth for any fabric that is delicate or intolerant of high heat.

Look into gods and goddesses of communication, such Hermes, Thoth, Iris, Oghma, and others. You could incorporate the symbols of those deities in the fabric print to add another layer of magickal protection to the case. For example, owls are protective creatures and associated with Athena, the Greek goddess of wisdom, making them a perfect design for a phone case.

1 Position the interfacing on the wrong side of the fabric so that it is ½" from the long edge and ½" from the top edge. Fold over fabric and press with a hot iron to fuse the fabric to the interfacing on both sides. Repeat with the other piece of fabric and interfacing.

2 Using a binder clip, clip the two case sides together. Sew around all three unfinished edges with a zipper foot. If you are using fabric that has a design that runs one way, make sure the side with the design running upright is facing in. This way, when you turn the phone case right-side out, you won't end up with the design upside down. Reinforce the beginning, ending, and corners of the seam by backstitching.

3 Carefully trim seams and clip corners.

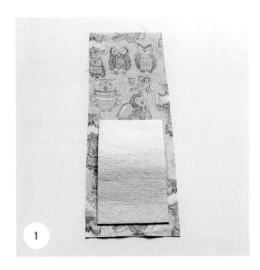

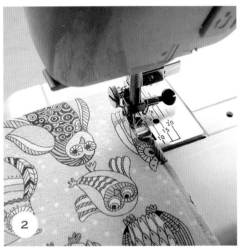

4   Use the steam setting on your iron to heat the phone case. This will make it easier to turn right-side out. Caution: the fabric will be hot! Use a chopstick or other turning tool to push out the corners.

5   Give the phone case one last pressing.

CHARGING

Burn an incense made from mint, orris root, parsley, yarrow, or yew (or a combination of these herbs) to access their properties of communication. If your intention for the case is one of protection from theft (whether physical or the hacking of your phone's contents), use an incense made from aspen, basil, cumin, dill, juniper, or tarragon (or, again, a combination).

Hold the phone case in the smoke of the incense and say the following:

Through the ether, as they go,
Let my words travel to and fro.
Let them bring naught but good to me,
No other to read them but who is meant to see.

Visualize a yellow glow encompassing the phone case, imbuing it with powers of clear communication and protection.

USB Holder

MATERIALS

8" × 3½" piece of fabric
6¾" × 3¼" piece of heavy-weight
   interfacing
Thread
Awl, skewer, or other sharp tool
2-part size 00 grommets or 2-part ¼"
   size eyelets
Split ring

DIFFICULTY

✄ ✄ ✄

TIME

1 hour

These days much of our life is conducted online or is computerized. Emails, work projects, schoolwork—all of it ends up as 1s and 0s. Many a witch keeps their Book of Shadows in a Word document or webpage. One computer crash or forgotten password can see all your handiwork disappear. So, in addition to practicing safe computing, keeping a backup is an easy way to protect your e-goods.

Increasing that protection with a USB carrier that attaches to your keychain is both practical and magickal.

The holder can be made out of any fabric, although linen is best suited for this project because it is made of flax, which has protective properties. However, use whatever fabric resonates with you. Colors such as white, black, and purple have protective energies. Prints that incorporate pentacles, solar crosses (or crosses in general), eyes, or the triquetra tap into the protective energies of those symbols. Also, prints that include protective plants and flowers such as holly, ivy, cactus, or thistle add another layer of intention to the holder.

This project is useful for using up scraps of fabric. It can also be matched to fabric for the phone case in the previous chapter as a way to double the protective aura around your digital presence.

1 On the wrong side of the fabric, fuse the interfacing so that it is ⅛" from the sides and the top of the fabric.

2 Fold fabric in half, lengthwise, right sides together

Leaving a gap keeps the seam allowances from becoming bulky.

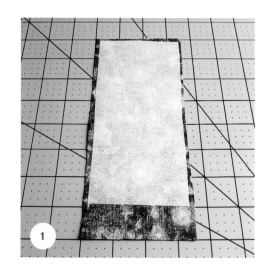

3　Sew a ⅛" seam from the top fold to the corner, then pivot to sew a ⅛" seam down the length of the fabric. Backstitch at the start and stop of the seam. If you catch a tiny bit of the interfacing when sewing, that's okay.

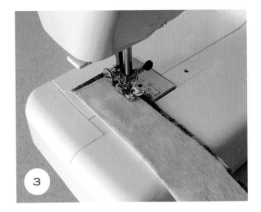

4　Using a chopstick or other turner tool, turn holder right-side out. Carefully push out the corners. Press.

5　Turn up the unstitched short side ½" and then ½" again. Use a ruler or hem gauge to measure the depth of the fold. Press.

6　Topstitch close to second fold. This seam helps reinforce the opening as well as keep the fabric from shifting.

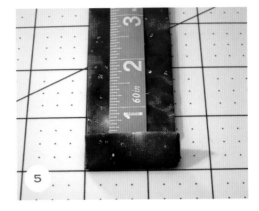

7　Fold up the stitched side 2½". Press.

8　Topstitch around all edges, and backstitch to secure the start and end points.

9　Using an awl, poke a hole at the top of the holder.

10　Attach grommets or eyelets according to the manufacturer's instructions.

11　Insert the split ring.

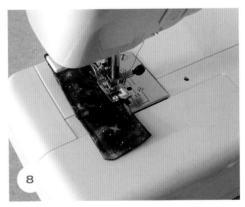

Using a heavy-duty needle makes sewing the outside edges easier.

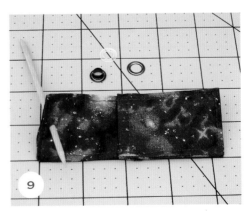

A bind rune created from the runes Algiz ᛉ (protection), Fehu ᚠ (mobile property), and Mannaz ᛗ (manifestation).

CHARGING

When you have finished your holder, charge it as follows during a full moon:

Using your dominant index finger, trace the bind rune to the left onto the holder. Place malachite or red jasper on top of the holder and say the following:

> *Fabric sheath of my design,*
> *Protect the ideas and works of my mind,*
> *The thumb drive, and all its content,*
> *From virus, hacker, or ill intent.*

Let the holder sit out under the full moon. You can start to use it the following day.

This holder is also sized to fit lip balm. Use it to keep a charmed lip balm at hand for when you need to be more eloquent when speaking, for health, or for beauty.

Sew Divine

*D*ivination is a key practice in witchcraft. There's nothing like peering into the bottom of a cup of tea to see what the leaves might have to say to make one feel especially "witchy." The projects in this section are meant to combine sewing and divination in ways that will enhance your practice.

The Tea-Stained Tarot cloth on page 185 is a quick and easy project, but there is power in its simplicity. By choosing herbs that resonate with your own intentions you can create a truly personal tool. The Felt Runes on page 187 are a different take on an ancient oracle. The time spent on making them attunes them with your own energy.

These items also make wonderful gifts. The Teapot Cozy on page 189, gifted with a selection of various magickal tea blends, is a thoughtful present for the oracle, green witch, or kitchen witch in your life.

THIS PROJECT
WILL LEAVE YOU WITH
EXTRA TEA-STAINED FABRIC.
THE EXTRA CAN BE USED TO
MAKE A WRAP TO HOLD AND
PROTECT TAROT CARDS OR TO
MAKE PROJECTS LIKE THE
TEAPOT COZY ON
PAGE 189.

Before chemical dyes became available, weavers and witches alike used herbs and natural ingredients to dye their fabric. Madder, walnuts, onion skins, and even oranges and Queen Anne's lace were all used. Natural dyes are making a comeback these days, and while dyeing is a topic that is outside the scope of this book, I think this project is a perfect introduction to the topic. For more information on all the things you can do with a few plants from your garden, check the bibliography for book recommendations on the topic.

The use of tea in a project for tarot cards might seem a bit odd. Tea leaves are used in a quite different form of divination on their own. However, it is just that connection that makes tea staining perfect for this project. Tea is a masculine plant, and when coupled with the feminine energy of mugwort, it gives you a balanced platform on which to read the tarot.

Tea staining works with any natural fiber fabric. While cotton is listed below, you can use linen, silk, or any other material that isn't synthetic. It works best with white or light-colored fabrics. However, if you have a length of black silk and are only interested in imbuing it with the properties of the tea and mugwort, feel free to give it a tea bath.

While mugwort is listed below, there are plenty of other herbs that also have divination properties. If you cannot get your hands on mugwort, or if you have a particular affinity for a different herb, feel free to substitute it in this project, keeping in mind that different herbs may alter the shade a bit. Do a test swatch before placing all your cloth into the dye. Alternative herbs include clove, goldenrod, ground ivy, lavender, lemongrass, nutmeg, orange, pine, poppy, rose, sage, star anise, thyme, willow, and yarrow.

TEA STAINING

1 In a large pot, bring 6 cups of water to a boil. Add the tea bags and mugwort. Remove from heat. Let steep for 15 minutes.

2 Strain the water, removing the tea bags and mugwort.

3 Rinse the fabric in warm water, wetting it thoroughly. Wring it out, removing as much excess water as possible.

Tea-Stained Tarot Cloth

MATERIALS

6 cups water plus 1 cup
12 black tea bags
1 tablespoon dried mugwort
¾ yard white cotton
2 cups distilled white vinegar
2 tablespoons salt
Thread

DIFFICULTY

TIME

1 hour

TEA IS ASSOCIATED WITH STRENGTH AND COURAGE, TWO TRAITS ONE NEEDS WHEN LOOKING INTO THE MURKY REALMS OF THE UNKNOWN VIA DIVINATION.

4 Place the fabric in the pot with the tea stain. For an even color, stir the fabric frequently deosil (clockwise). As you stir, say,

Mugwort, witches' herb, imbue this fabric with your power.

See the divinatory energy of the mugwort seeping into every fiber of the fabric. The fabric can be soaked for only a few minutes for a light tint, or it can be left overnight for an even darker shade. To get an uneven dye pattern, use a small container—for example, a large mug or small bowl—and crumple up the fabric.

5 Once the desired shade has been achieved, pull out the fabric, rinse it with clear water, and wring out any excess.

6 In a bowl, mix 2 cups vinegar, 1 cup water, and 2 tablespoons salt. Add the fabric and allow it to soak for 15 minutes. This will set the color.

7 Once again rinse the fabric in clean water. Line or machine dry.

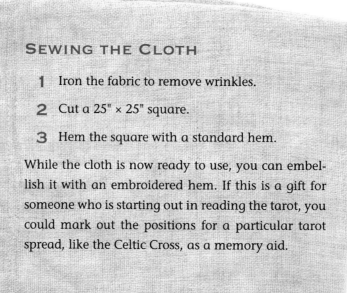

SEWING THE CLOTH

1 Iron the fabric to remove wrinkles.

2 Cut a 25" × 25" square.

3 Hem the square with a standard hem.

While the cloth is now ready to use, you can embellish it with an embroidered hem. If this is a gift for someone who is starting out in reading the tarot, you could mark out the positions for a particular tarot spread, like the Celtic Cross, as a memory aid.

Felt Runes

My first divination tool was a set of glass stones etched with runes. They had been a gift from a friend who had picked them up at a Renaissance festival. And while they sparked my interest in runes, I used them only once. The feel of the glass was all wrong. The etching was light in areas, making them hard to read. And they were too similar to the little counters I used when playing Magic: The Gathering for me to take seriously.

Over the years I primarily used tarot cards, but I always turned back to runes for spells and rituals. It wasn't until a couple of years ago, when my husband started making rune sets from wood, that I came back to the idea of having and using a set of my own. I'm not a woodworker, and I wanted to make my own set, so I turned to my sewing room for inspiration. This came in the form of a small bag filled with wool felt scraps from another project.

Over the course of a couple of nights, I created my first set. I used black felt because that is what I had on hand, and red embroidery thread because it contrasted well. You are welcome to use any color combination you wish. You might check out the color correspondences in the appendix for inspiration.

Polyester felt can be used as well; however, I have found it has a different feel and doesn't have the same weight as wool felt. On the other hand, polyester felt comes in many more colors than wool.

This is a good project for a winter weekend, when you can channel the energies of the north, quiet, and introspection into the runes. As you stitch, contemplate the various meanings of each rune. Consider not only the interpretation assigned to them but also any personal understanding you have for each. You can find a list of the Elder Futhark on page 48. When you have finished, make a pouch to hold the runes using the designs in the previous section, It's in the Bag.

If you don't like how a rune looks when you stitch it, you can easily pull out the thread and try again.

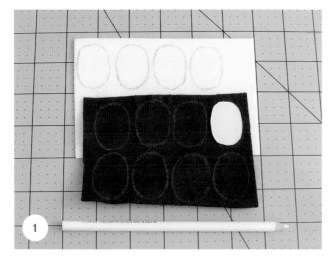

1. Using tracing paper, trace the rune pattern on page 246. Transfer the pattern to a piece of cardstock to make the template.

2. Using the template, draw 24 ovals onto the craft-weight interfacing. Cut the ovals out.

3. Using the template, draw 48 ovals onto the felt. Use a white or yellow colored pencil if the felt is dark colored. Cut on the outside of the lines on the felt and on the inside of the lines of the interfacing so that the interfacing is slightly smaller than the felt.

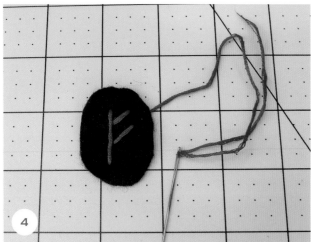

4. On 24 of the felt ovals, embroider the runes. Draw them first if you want. Use straight stitches for each stroke.

5. With the runes facing up, sandwich the interfacing ovals between a rune felt and a backing felt.

6. Using a whip stitch, encase the interfacing in the felt with embroidery thread. Sew only through the felt, taking care not to catch the interfacing in the needle. You can pull on the felt to give you room to work the needle and thread around the interfacing.

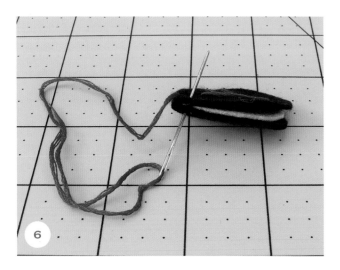

Once you have made your runes, consecrate them for your use.

If the runes are meant as a gift, cleanse them before giving them away, as you have handled the materials extensively.

ALTERNATIVE PROJECTS

These runes can be adapted for other uses, such as witch or oracle stones or amulets. For other oracle stones, simply embroider the symbols you want on the felt. To make an amulet, poke a hole through the top of the finished oval and push a jump ring through the hole. Thread a cord through the jump ring.

Tea plays a part in my rituals and spellcasting. Sometimes, a cup of tea is the entirety of the spell. I grow lemon balm and chamomile in my garden and collect wood sorrel, creeping Charlie, and dandelion, among other wildflowers, for my teas.

I didn't always have a love of tea. In my youth I drank Mountain Dew by the bucket. I never got into the coffee habit but eventually moved onto powdered drinks for my caffeine intake. It wasn't until my late thirties that I began to appreciate tea on its own, and then as a way to practice my craft. I have a favorite mug, teapot, and infuser, and it was only a matter of time before I started thinking about sewing projects to enhance my tea rituals.

Tea has volumes of tradition—magick and otherwise—attached to it. There are ceremonies attached to its making, myths and legends to its components, and a vast lore to the beverage. One of the easiest ways to incorporate the essences of herbs is through a cup of tea. You can divine your future through the leaves. You can use the steam as a makeshift incense. The versatility of tea makes it one of the most useful tools in a witch's inventory.

To that end, why not pay as much attention to the accoutrements used in enjoying your cup of tea? Not only in your choice of mug and teapot but in the paraphernalia: the coaster under your mug and the cozy on your pot.

You can add all manner of magick symbols to your teapot cozy, helping amplify the energy of your work. These symbols can be placed on the inside of the cozy if you want to be circumspect.

The teapot cozy and the following coaster are so quick and easy to make you could make several, suited for various magickal purposes. Or whip up a set as a gift for a tea-loving friend. They don't use much fabric, so they are perfect for clearing out the scraps in your stash.

You do not want the cozy to cover the handle or spout, so just measure the width of the body.

Teapot Cozy

MATERIALS

Exterior fabric the size of your A measurement plus 5" × your B measurement

Lining fabric the size of A plus 5" × B

Cotton batting the size of A × B

Thread to match

2 buttons

DIFFICULTY

✂ ✂ ✂

TIME

1 hour

MEASUREMENTS AND MATH

A   Measure around the teapot from the bottom of the lid on one side, around the bottom of the teapot, and back up to the bottom of the lid on the other side. This is your A measurement.

B   Measure from the back of the teapot to the front where the spout starts. This is your B measurement.

B

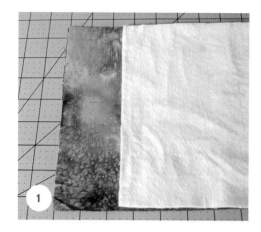

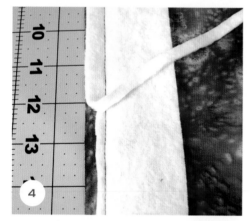

1 Lay the exterior fabric wrong-side down, right side facing out, on your workspace. Place the lining right-side down on top of the exterior piece. Position the batting on top of the lining 2½" from either side of the short ends of the rectangle. Once you turn the cozy right-side out, the batting will be sandwiched between the two pieces of fabric.

2 Pin all three layers together.

3 Starting at the middle of one long side, sew a ½" seam around all edges, leaving a 2" gap for turning. Backstitch at both the start and end of the stitching.

4 Trim the corners and the batting on the long sides to reduce bulk. Turn the cozy right-side out. Press.

5 Topstitch around all the edges, closing the opening. This helps secure the batting.

6 Mark the buttonholes ¾" from the top and ¾" in from the sides. Make the buttonholes ¼" longer than your buttons. So, for example, if your buttons are 1", the buttonholes should be 1¼" long.

7 *If machine sewing:* Sew the buttonholes and open them with a seam ripper. *If hand sewing:* Make the buttonholes by cutting through all layers of the cozy the width you marked. Using thread and needle, whip stitch around the edge of the buttonhole through all layers.

8 Fold the cozy in half and mark button placement. Sew the buttons.

Brew a pot of tea. Place the cozy around the teapot. Enjoy!

Make sure to use the buttonhole foot on your machine.

For even more magickal oomph, check
out the correspondence appendix at the
end of the book and coordinate the fabric
and thread color with your herb choice.

Scented Coasters

MATERIALS

2 pieces of fabric, 10" × 5"
2 pieces of cotton batting, 5" × 5"
Thread in a coordinating color
½ teaspoon herbs of choice

DIFFICULTY

TIME

1 hour

The heat from your mug will warm the herbs in the coaster, releasing their scent. It's a subtle way of working magick out in the open if you need to be discreet (like brewing a cup of peppermint tea when you want to harness the plant's protective properties without alerting those around you).

This project makes one circular coaster and one square coaster at the same time.

1 Using tracing paper, trace the pattern piece for the circle coaster on page 247. Cut it out.

2 Fold the 10" × 5" fabric in half to make a square. Use the circle pattern piece to cut out 2 pieces from the fabric and 1 piece from the batting. Cut the second 10" × 5" rectangle in half to make two 5" × 5" squares.

3 Sprinkle your herbs evenly onto each piece of batting, keeping them in the middle and making sure they stay inside the seam allowances.

4 Place a piece of fabric wrong-side down, right side facing out, on the batting. Place the second piece of fabric right-side down on top of the first piece. Pin all three layers together. When you turn the coasters right-side out, the batting and herbs will be sandwiched between the fabric.

5 Sew a ¼" seam through all thicknesses, leaving a space for turning, backstitching at the start and stop of the seam.

6 Clip the curves of the circle coaster. Trim the corners of the square coaster.

7 Turn the coasters right-side out. Turn the edges of the openings under and press the coasters. Pressing keeps the unfinished edges in place until you finish them—and makes your sewing space smell good.

8 Topstitch the square coaster, closing the opening. Topstitch a center square. For the circle, topstitch around the edge, closing the opening. Continue topstitching a spiral ¼" from the edge until you reach the center.

Use the edge of your presser foot as a guide while topstitching the spiral.

PSYCHIC TEA RECIPE

Tea is an excellent way to incorporate the powers of herbs into your magickal practice. Use the following recipe to make up a batch of psychic tea for use the next time you engage in divination rituals.

Mix the dried herbs listed below together and store them in a glass jar with a tight-fitting lid. To make a cup of tea, steep 1 heaping teaspoon of the mix in 1 cup boiling water for 5 minutes. Breathe in the aroma and let the plants open you to messages from the universe.

½ cup dried mugwort
¼ cup dried orange peel
¼ cup dried cinnamon chips
⅛ cup whole cloves
⅛ cup dried ginger root

Scrappy Magick

Witches and sewists alike are loath to waste even the smallest of scraps. They are pragmatic people who will have a small (or large) hoard of jars, cardboard, or fabric scraps on hand "just in case." The advent of Pinterest, with its millions of artfully photographed craft tutorials, just exacerbates that issue. And while the sheer potential of all those button bins and bits of lace is exciting, there's a time for planning and a time for creating.

It's not just a matter of waste not, want not, however. Scrap crafting engages our being in ways that sewing doesn't. The act of creating something from scraps that would normally be thrown away touches on the witch's conservation and frugality. This is an aspect of the Crone, who sees potential in even the humblest of materials. The Crone knows that landfills don't need yet another bag of cotton odds and ends. She uses her great knowledge to find new uses for what others would discard.

Using up scraps in projects taps into the witch's creativity. There are hundreds of projects and ideas in the world one can use. This is an aspect of the Maiden and her boundless ingenuity. The Maiden brings a new perspective to every endeavor. Not burdened with preconceived notions, she approaches projects with enthusiasm and a desire to try new things.

Finally, making an item whose purpose is decorative ties the witch directly to spirit. The witch knows that just as their body needs nourishment, so too does their soul. The Mother balances the pragmatism of the Crone with the exuberance of the Maiden. She serves meals on beautiful dishes and tucks her children into bed under soft quilts. The Mother reminds us to stop and smell the roses from time to time.

The following projects make use of all the leftover bits of fabric. The results can then be used in a variety of ways both mundane and magickal. Perhaps add a new activity to your spring traditions: spring crafting. After a long winter of stockpiling and sorting yarn, beads, and scraps, open the windows, let the fresh air come in, and make something new out of the old.

1. Cut your fabric scraps into strips. You can stick with rectangles or try some of the tapered shapes shown here for different finished bead shapes.

2. With the wrong side of the fabric facing up, place the skewer on one short end.

3. Start to roll the fabric around the skewer. Make sure the fabric is rolled tightly.

4. Place some glue on the fabric strip and continue rolling. Keep rolling the fabric tightly around the skewer, adding some glue every few rolls. The glue hardens the bead, so feel free to use it liberally.

5. Add glue to the end of the strip. Roll to the end, pressing firmly to secure it.

6. Remove the bead from the skewer.

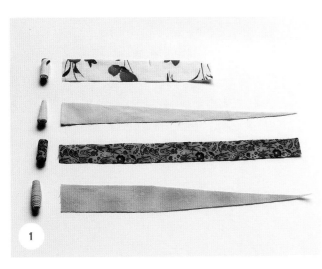

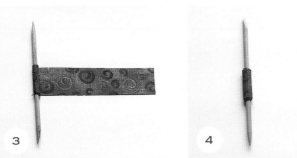

Fabric Beads

MATERIALS
Fabric scraps
Glue stick
Wooden skewer

DIFFICULTY

TIME
15 minutes

The process of turning fabric scraps into beads is deceptively simple. The first time I tried it, I ended up finding myself with a dozen done in less than 10 minutes. I didn't have a plan for them; I had just wanted to see what was involved.

These beads can be made using any fabric. For very fine or slippery fabric, you can add an iron-on interfacing first as a stabilizer. Use strips of fabric around 1" or smaller. Wider strips tend to be more difficult to work with. While the instructions include a wooden skewer, anything cylindrical can be used: straws, knitting needles, pencils, dried spaghetti—anything you don't mind getting glue on. The size of the rolling tool you use will change the diameter of the bead hole.

When you have finished your beads, you can immediately use them as is. You can also finish them with a sealer if you wish. Or embellish them further with embroidery thread and seed beads.

Set aside an afternoon and make up a basket of beads to use for garlands, witch ladders, jewelry, and embellishments. This is a great project to do with children, as it is simple and helps develop hand-eye coordination.

Fabric Twine

MATERIALS

Strips of fabric no wider than 1"

DIFFICULTY

TIME

1 hour

Spinning thread by hand is no longer a routine chore. With the exception of dedicated crafters, spinning has become a job for machines. Once, though, spinning was a major occupation, especially for women. Hand-held drop spindles even allowed for one to spin while walking, making for a quite different take on the mobile app.

While the machines do their job very well, there are opportunities to spin our own cording out of our scrap bags. Twisting scraps into lengths of twine provides witches with another way to reduce waste and create materials for more crafts and rituals. Fabric twine can be used in a number of projects, including witch's cords, rugs, coasters, garlands, and embroidery. Use it to make the Altar Bowls on page 101.

Any non-stretch fabric can be used to make cording, although thick fabric might take a bit more wrist strength. Fabrics that fray easily, like taffeta, silk, and polyesters, will result in a fuzzier twine than cotton will. It is easier to roll the cord with wet fingertips, so keep a damp sponge nearby (or if you aren't too fussy, lick your fingertips like I do).

The activity lends itself to a group setting. If you are part of a coven, perhaps you can all make twine, knit, or quilt while raising creative energy together.

1 To keep the strips from ending at the same place, start with one strip that is slightly longer than the other. Knot the two strips of fabric together at one end.

2 Hold the knot in your non-dominant hand. Take the strip of fabric that is farthest from your body and roll it between your thumb and index finger away from you.

3 Bring the rolled strip toward you, over the non-twisted strip.

4 Take the non-twisted strip, which is now the fabric farthest way from your body and roll it between your fingers away from you.

5 Repeat steps 3 and 4. When you reach the last 1" of a strip of fabric, feed in a new strip like this: When the strip end is away from you, lay a new strip over it, overlapping the ends. Roll them together and then bring them over the strip close to you. Continue on.

6 When you have used up all your fabric strips, knot the end of the twine.

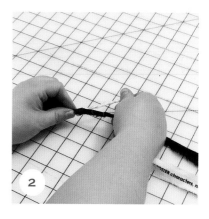

Fabric Flowers

MATERIALS
Scraps of fabric
Thread
Polyester stuffing
Embroidery thread
Buttons or beads

DIFFICULTY

TIME
30 minutes

Flowers are a common offering and altar decoration for many rituals and holidays. For those who have allergies or don't have access to fresh flowers, I offer up this project.

This project uses fabric scraps, buttons, and floss, along with a little polyester stuffing to create three-dimensional flowers. Use them for altar decorations, garlands, or Beltane or other spring, love, or prosperity spellwork. You can add a pinch of ground herbs corresponding with your intent when you add the stuffing to enhance the flowers' magickal energy.

1   Using tracing paper, trace the patterns for the fabric flowers on page 248.

2   Cut out as many pieces of fabric as you like.

3   Baste around the edge of the circle ¼" away from the edge.

4   Pull on the thread ends, gathering the circle opening slightly together. Place a small ball of polyester stuffing (about as much as you can fit in your hand) into the opening and then resume pulling on the threads to close the opening.

5   Tie the ends of the thread together and trim off the excess thread.

6   Thread an embroidery needle with 6 strands of floss.

7   Push the needle through the opening in the back and out the middle of the front of the flower ball, leaving a tail of about 3 inches of floss out the back. Push the needle again through the back opening and out the center of the front, pulling the thread tight. You've made the first petal section. (Don't be alarmed: the first petal section always looks a little wonky.)

8   Repeat the above step 4 more times, forming 5 petals in the flower. Tie off the floss with the tail.

9   Attach 2 buttons—1 at the front and 1 at the back—to the center of the flower, using 6 strands of embroidery floss. Pull the floss tight. Tie off the floss at the back of the flower.

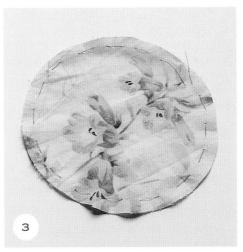

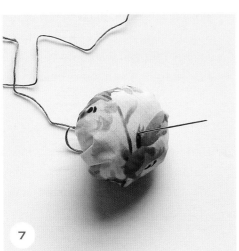

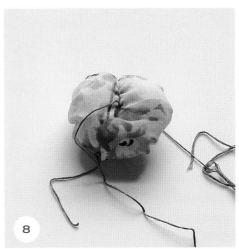

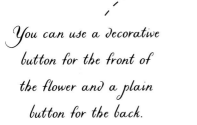

You can use a decorative button for the front of the flower and a plain button for the back.

Beltane Flower Garland

MATERIALS
3 yards red ribbon
3 yards white ribbon
3 yards yellow ribbon
12 fabric flowers (see page 200)
Dried herbs or essential oils
Thread

DIFFICULTY

TIME
1 hour

For the following garland, first make twelve fabric flowers using the steps on pages 200–201. Make them in shades of green, red, white, and yellow.

When you add the polyester stuffing, add a pinch of one or more of the following dried herbs: rose, rosemary, or lilac. Alternatively, skip the dried herbs and instead anoint each flower with a drop of one or more of the following essential oils: passion flower, tuberose, or vanilla.

1 Braid the 3 ribbons together. Make a loop at each end of the braid.

2 Sew the flowers onto the braid, spacing them evenly along the length of the braid.

3 As you work, think upon the mysteries of springtime: the reunion of Demeter and Persephone, the union of the Goddess and God, the new life rising all around you, the sense of fresh possibilities. Think about the scent of rich earth; the song of the birds; the taste of the first greens, rhubarb and radishes, all the produce that is now in season; the sight of flowers in bloom; and the feel of the warming sun on your skin. Use all these to raise spring energy that you work into your garland. Visualize it radiating a joyful energy. Say,

> *Spring has sprung, the cold is done, prosperity comes, it's time for fun.*

4 Hang your garland over or on your altar on Beltane. Leave it up until Midsummer to tap into the fertility and prosperity magick stored in it.

*This flower garland is a great
craft to make with children: from
placing the flowers to braiding the
cord, it gets them involved preparing
for the Beltane celebration.*

Prosperity Sachets

MATERIALS

Pouch (see page 162 for materials and
    instructions)
Embroidery thread
Herbs of choice
Stones of choice

DIFFICULTY

TIME

1 hour

Sachets aren't just for linens. Combine herbs, stones, and symbols to make a powerful amulet for success and prosperity. Slip them into the pockets of the clothes you're to wear to an interview. You can even make a sachet to tumble in the dryer with your work clothes, harnessing the passion of fire and creativity of air to add further power to your magick. The possibilities are only limited by your imagination.

1 Use the instructions on page 162 to make a pouch. Look in the correspondences table in the appendix to find colors that relate to specific prosperity issues. Green fabric is good for economic prosperity. Yellow is well suited for educational prosperity. Match the fabric type to your intention, as well. Linen is associated with properties of wealth and prosperity. Cotton is associated with the earth element, placing it in the domain of wealth. And silk has a cachet of affluence that could be used to reinforce the prosperity energies of the sachet.

2 Consider embroidering symbols of success on the outside of the pouch. If your sachet is meant to bring you wealth, you could simply embroider a dollar sign or other currency sign. Or, if you want to tap into a form that has a more mystical pedigree, consider using bind runes.

   Bind runes are combinations of two or more runes that merge their individual meanings into a more complex symbol. Embroider one of the runes on the next page onto the sachets in orange, yellow, green, gold, and silver threads. Or combine individual runes into your own personal bind rune.

   If your work, or the company you have an interview with, has a logo or promotional items (T-shirts, tote bags, etc.) and you are looking to find success there, include them in the sachets.

3 Include herbs for success, such as lemon balm, cinnamon, clove, and ginger. Also add herbs for wealth, such as allspice, basil, chamomile, clover, mint, and nutmeg.

4 And give your sachet a final boost by adding aventurine, citrine, jade, pyrite, or quartz crystal.

5 Tie up your prosperity sachet securely (especially if you will use it in the dryer). Then carry it with you wherever you could use extra prosperous energies.

Personal Wealth or Financial Security

Success in Speaking and Writing

Realization of Ambition

Success in Business

Success in Legal Action

Success in Risk-Taking

Witch Cords

MATERIALS
1 yard of string or cord

DIFFICULTY
✂ ✂ ✂

TIME
1 hour

Witch cords are well-documented magick tools. In their creation magick intent, or power, is knotted into a length of string. It is a practice that takes something linear and simple and transforms it, tying it into an intention. String on its own is not a particularly useful item. Only when it is woven, braided, or used to bind something is its potential fulfilled. In a very real sense, tying a knot is a bit of magick just on its own.

Typically, witch cords are tied with nine knots, with a part of the spell spoken with each knot. Like witch ladders, cord magick has been used historically for hexes. However, that isn't its only use.

Sir James Frazer notes many examples of knot magick in his book The Golden Bough. The knots, used as charms, magick, and ritual, relate to a variety of themes. Knots can be used to bind, to harm, and to cure, and they can even have an influence on weddings, especially the honeymoon. Further, Raven Grimassi notes that J. B. Andrews "reports that witches use three cords to invoke aid from the stars; one black, one red, and one white. The cords are knotted for various purposes, and pins are inserted into the knots to fix the spell in place."

Knot magick is one of the simplest of all magicks to perform. This can lead to it being overlooked or dismissed as simplistic (as if all magick must involve candles, salts, crystals, and other accoutrements in order to be effective). If you keep in mind it is the Will of the witch that is the force behind a spell, you come to appreciate simple spells that can be performed on the fly.

Witch cords can be made from any number of materials: ribbons, thread, yarn, fancy cords from craft stores, and even fabric selvages. If you made the Fabric Twine on page 198, you can use it for this spell. You can match the color of the string to your purpose: red for love spells, orange for legal matters, brown for healing, and so on.

1 Lay your cord on the middle of your altar. Around the cord place the following:

Above: Stone for earth, particularly one that corresponds with your spell intentions

Right: Incense that corresponds with the goal of your spell

Below: White tea light candle

Left: Small bowl or cup of water

2 Cast a circle according to your practice. Invite any deities or spirit helpers you work with to join you.

3 Light the incense and candle. Take up the cord. Pass the cord through the smoke of the incense and say,

Air, I call on you to begin my spell.

Pass the cord above the candle flame—high enough that it won't catch fire—and say,

Fire, I call on you to intensify my spell.

Touch your fingers to the water and then touch the cord, wetting it slightly. Say,

Water, I call on you to set my spell in motion.

Finally, touch it to the stone and say,

Earth, I call on you to grow my spell.

4 Sit with the cord in your lap. You will be tying the knots in this order:

Knot 1 at the far left end
Knot 2 at the far right end
Knot 3 four inches in from knot 1
Knot 4 four inches in from knot 2
Knot 5 four inches in from knot 3
Knot 6 four inches in from knot 4
Knot 7 four inches in from knot 5
Knot 8 four inches in from knot 6
Knot 9 in the middle of the cord

5 As you tie the knots say the following:

Knot of One, my will be done.
Knot of Two, my spell comes true.
Knot of Three, my goal I'll see.
Knot of Four, my power grows more.
Knot of Five, my magick thrives.
Knot of Six, my intention is fixed.
Knot of Seven, my purpose is driven.
Knot of Eight, my call to fate.
Knot of Nine, my aims align.

6 Once finished, thank whatever deities or spirit helpers you invited in, and then close the circle. Keep the cord in a spell bag someplace safe. Alternatively, if the spell is something you are sure you will never want undone, bury or burn it so that the knots can never be untied.

ALTERNATE USES

Witch cords and knot magick have also been used to "tie up" power and energies to save for later use. Instead of the chant in the above spell, you can instead invoke energies of elements, directions, spirits, deities, or what have you as you make your knots. This will store that power into the cord. When you have need for that energy in spellwork, you can untie the knot to call it forth.

Witch Ladder

MATERIALS

½ yard cording

Cotton thread

Materia magica

DIFFICULTY

TIME

1 hour

Like witch cords, a witch ladder is a method of containing and directing a spell. Historically, it was made with feathers tied or woven into string. While its original purpose was usually for hexing, that's not the goal for this project. It instead takes the process and theory behind witch ladders to make a powerful spell talisman for your use.

In her book Sewing Bits and Pieces, Sandi Henderson suggests saving squares of fabric from various projects to use to make her Saturday Market Skirt, the idea being one of creating a piece of sartorial history. This was the inspiration for my first witch ladder. As a seamstress, I work on dozens of commissions each year, as well as personal projects and crafts to sell. With my head bent over my sewing machine, it can be hard to get a sense of just how much work I have done. This witch ladder provided a record of all I had accomplished through the scraps of fabric, leftover buttons, ribbon, lace, and other notions I saved.

My witch ladders act as powerful talismans. Since all my sewing involves magick in some way, each bit on the ladders carries a piece of that energy. Stringing them together brings that combined magick into one place, amplifying it as each piece of materia magica builds on the other. As the majority of my sewing is currently concerned with making money, my ladders are dedicated to my economic prosperity. When they are hung where I can see them, not only am I reminded of the hard work I have already done, but my attention releases the magick stored in them into the world.

Start by collecting scraps of fabric, thread, yarn, and so on. These will act as the "feathers" of the witch ladder. These can come from anywhere: past projects, old clothes, remnants from the craft store. You'll want to match the scraps to the ladder's purpose. Making a ladder intended to battle insecurity and to boost your self-esteem? A mix of scraps from clothes you've worn before but no longer wear and fabric bought just for this purpose will do. Is your ladder going to be one to bring love into your life? Use red and pink yarn and fabric, along with loose threads taken from your clothes.

Add buttons, charms, beads, and any other embellishments to your pile of materials. These will act not only as enhancers for your spell, adding in the element of spirit, but on a practical level they will help the ladder hang true. The notions should be matched with the ladder's intent. Pins and needles can be added in for a ladder meant to repel negative attention or energies. For a ladder to bring wealth, use gold- and silver-toned buttons, green lace, or charms shaped as money. If you are making a ladder to target a specific person (for example, to aid in healing of a friend), use a button from the person's clothing to tie it to them.

Take your time gathering your materia magica. The witch ladder is magick made physical and as such needs extra care and preparation. You want to only use materials that are completely in tune with your intended spell. Think about how you want the materials to hang on the ladder, in what order you will attach them, and how the finished spell will look. You can even sketch out the plan in your Book of Shadows or your spell journal. Until you are ready, keep your materials in a spell bag. A simple pouch will do.

You will also need a piece of string or cord ½ yard in length. If you made the Fabric Twine found on page 198, you can use that. To attach the fabric and embellishments to the string, use cotton thread in a color that corresponds with your intention.

1   Once you have your materials, give them a moon bath under a new moon. Place the spell bag out where moonlight will fall on it. Ask the moon to cleanse the materials of any energies that are not aligned with your purpose. Be specific about what that purpose is, saying something like this:

    New Moon, shining down, let your light cleanse these items of all energies that are not aligned with [your purpose].

2   See the light of the new moon shining down and gently cleansing all your materials. See them glowing with a soft, white light, ready for use.

3   To make your witch ladder, sit with your materials gathered. Cast a circle according

to your practice. Invite whatever deities and spirits you work with to join you.

4   Lay out the cord, thread, and all your materials before you. Take up the cord and say,

    This, the foundation of my spell.

    Cut a piece of thread and tie your first piece of fabric or embellishment to the cord, saying,

    This, to make my will manifest.

    Tie the piece to the cord nine inches from the top. As you tie the knots, visualize what your spell is to accomplish and how this piece contributes to that goal.

5   Take your second piece of the ladder and tie it to the cord about three inches below the first. Say,

    This, to make my will manifest.

    Repeat this with every piece of the ladder. Expand on it if you want, specifying what your will is, how a particular piece will accomplish that, or how you envision the success of your spell. Talk to those deities and spirits you have invited in, asking them to lend their energy to your spell.

6   Continue until you have added the last item to the ladder. Once you have finished, say,

    This is my will; it is done.

    Thank those you have called in to help. Close your circle.

7   Hang the ladder from the ceiling in an east-facing corner where it won't touch anything. Keep the ladder dust free. For as long as the spell is to work, keep it hanging. If your spell is results orientated, such as a spell to bring money, take it down once the spell has worked. After you take it down, pull the ladder apart, thanking each component as you do. Once you have dismantled the ladder, bury all the components.

HERBS FOR INTENTIONS

Friendship: Acacia, heather, lemon, passionflower, sweetpea, thyme, yarro

Familial Love: Barley, cinnamon, primrose, rosemary, sorrel, vervain, will

Romantic Love: Basil, catnip, daisy, lavender, rose, patchouli, vanilla, viol

1 Using tracing paper, trace the pattern piece for the heart on page 246. Cut it out.

2 Make a template by tracing the pattern onto a piece of thin cardboard. A file folder or cereal box works well for this.

3 Make 2 felt hearts by tracing the template onto the felt. Cut out the felt hearts.

4 Leave the hearts plain or decorate them as you like. Beads in colors that correspond with your magickal intentions, as well as other decorative notions, can be used.

5 Place 1 felt heart on top of the other. Using a whip stitch, sew the hearts together with embroidery thread, leaving an opening for stuffing and your chosen herbs. If this heart is for someone in particular, envision each stitch binding you both closer together in love, friendship, and so on. If the heart is for yourself as part of a spell to bring love into your life, envision the stitches bringing that love ever closer.

6 Slip in a small amount of stuffing and a pinch of the herbs. Close the opening.

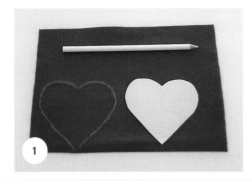

Heart Charm

MATERIALS
Felt scraps in any color, at least 4" square
Embroidery thread
Stuffing
Herbs appropriate to your intention

DIFFICULTY

TIME
30 minutes

The sheer number of love and love-related spells in magick practices is truly impressive. It seems that matters of the heart have been a priority of spellcraft from the first days of magick. The felt project presented here is a play on that long history of love spells: hearts cut from felt and stuffed with herbs to be given to friends and lovers as charms to strengthen the love between the two of you.

These hearts can also be used in spells. Perhaps you are performing magick to bring love into your life. You can make a red heart filled with dried rose petals. Make the heart the focus of your spell and then carry it with you as a charm. In ritual, hearts of various colors and filled with different herbs can invoke a plethora of energies, from passion to healing to parental love.

The hearts can be embroidered, beaded, and dressed up with buttons and other notions. You can use pens and paint to decorate them as well. A ribbon loop can be added so they can be hung. The possibilities for enhancing their magickal uses are endless.

Appendix

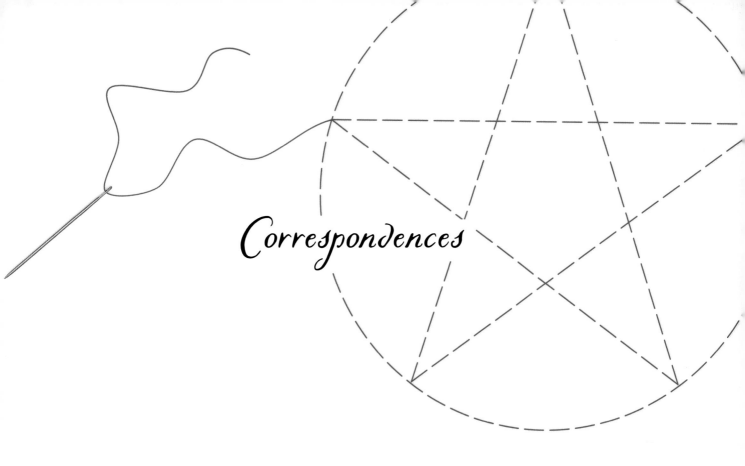

Correspondences

ARTS AND CRAFTS DEITIES

The following list is a brief overview of the many gods and goddesses who have areas of interest in sewing, crafting, and artistry. It is by no means exhaustive. It is shared as a jumping-off point for you to find deities to work with in your sewing spellcraft. Before choosing to work with a certain god or goddess, research them. Read all you can about their mythology, about the culture they come from (especially if it is a culture to which you don't belong). Meditate and journey to meet with them and see if they are interested in working with you. If so, great. If not, look for divine aid elsewhere.

Abe-Mango: An Incan goddess who taught humans how to cook, weave cloth, and make pottery. She can be invoked for weaving-related projects, kitchen-related crafts, or fire-related crafts.

Al-Kutbay: The Nabataean god of knowledge, commerce, writing, and prophecy. Invoke him for projects related to divination and for business success.

Ame-No-Tanabata-Hime-No-Mikoto: The Shinto goddess of weavers. Call on her for love projects and projects revering the departed

Ananse: The West African spider god. He can be called on for projects that involve spinning or knot work.

Anulap: The Truk Island god of magick and knowledge. He can be invoked for any projects that are related to magick: pouches, oracles mats, altar cloths, and so on.

Apollo: The Greek god of fine arts, medicine, music, and poetry. Invoke him for projects related to music and poetry, as well as when making medicine pouches. You can also call on him when you need to include sun energy in your projects.

Arachne: A Roman weaver transformed by the goddess Athena into a spider. Call on her when working on projects related to self-confidence, self-expression, and weaving.

Athena: The Greek goddess and patron goddess of spinners and other forms of handiwork. Invoke her for projects meant to bolster courage and leadership or for protective works. Any projects featuring owls or related to knowledge also benefit from her attention.

Brighid: A Celtic goddess and patron deity of poetry, smithing, medicine, arts and crafts, cattle and other livestock, and sacred wells. She can be invoked for projects related to healing, projects that involve metal adornment (including metallic embroidery threads), and decorative crafts.

Cerridwen: The Celtic goddess of rebirth, transformation, and inspiration. Invoke her for projects involved with transformation, especially clothes meant to help one manifest a particular energy (confidence, psychic abilities, abundance, spiritual progress, etc.).

Creidhne: The Irish god of art, particularly goldsmithing, as well as bronze, brass, and silver. Invoke him for projects involving metallic decoration, thread, or even colors (gold, silver, brass, copper, etc.).

Enki: The Sumerian god of crafts, water, intelligence, and creation. Call on him to bring water energy to projects, for decorative crafts, and especially for projects that include his sacred number, forty.

Goibhniu (aka Gobniu): The Irish god of hospitality and smithing. Invoke him in projects for guests or for welcome: blankets and throws, guest towels, decorations. His Welsh counterpart is Govannon.

Gratiae: Roman goddesses, personifications of grace and beauty. Call on them for projects that are to be worn in the hair or meant to beautify the wearer.

Hephaestus: The Greek god of blacksmiths, craftsmen, artisans, and sculptors. Invoke his aid for projects involving metal buttons, trims, or decorations; installing zippers, hooks and eyes, snaps, and other metal fastenings; or projects that involve drafting patterns by hand or that involve complex construction.

Hestia: The Greek goddess of the hearth, home, architecture, domesticity, family, and the state. Call on her for projects related to household items, especially those that are meant for the comfort and well-being of family and friends: throws, pillows, slippers, robes (non-ceremonial), and so on.

Hulda: A Norse goddess spinning and specifically the cultivating of flax. It is said that she taught how to spin flax into fabric. When you are using linen or when you are working on projects that involve weaving, call on her to lend her expertise.

Ixnextli: The Aztec Goddess of weavers. Invoke her when working on weaving projects.

Kabta: The Mesopotamian/Sumerian god of artisans. Call on him for projects meant to be used in or to adorn the house.

Klotho (aka Clotho): The Greek Goddess of spinning and one of the three Fates. Invoke her aid on projects that are time sensitive.

Luchta: The Irish god of art. You can call on him for projects meant for protection or attack: power pouches, protective charms, and so on.

Lugh (aka Lug): The Celtic god of fire, metallurgy, crafting, and weaving. He is called upon for projects that involve weaving, knitting, crochet, macramé, or any embroidery or for projects related to Lughnasadh.

Metis: The Greek Oceanid of wisdom, deep thought, and cunning. She can be invoked for projects related to water, for magick pouches related to wisdom or cunning, or when imbuing those qualities in clothes. She may also be called upon for projects related to problem-solving.

Minerva: The Roman goddess of wisdom and patron deity of arts, trade, strategy, poetry, medicine, crafts, and magick. Invoke her for projects that involve magick (spell pouches, protective charms, etc.) and general crafting. If you make handicrafts to sell, call on her aid to make them appealing to potential customers.

The Muses: Greek goddesses of inspiration in the arts, sciences, and literature. Invoke them when you need inspiration in your crafting.

Nabu: The Assyrian and Babylonian god of wisdom, writing, fertility, water, and vegetation. Ask for his aid in projects involving fertility or divination or when making writing-related items like journal covers.

Nidaba: The Sumerian goddess of writing, learning, the harvest, and organization. Call on her for any new project that you are creating from a pattern, baskets and bags (for holding groceries and goods), or projects that are meant for organization, such as sewing baskets, tool rolls, and so on.

Oghma: The Irish god of communication and writing and the inventor of the Ogham alphabet. He is also the patron deity of poets. Invoke his aid in projects related to writing, like alphabet samplers, for inspiration, or when writing down instructions for making a project.

Orunmila: The orisha of wisdom, knowledge, and divination. You can call on him for projects involved in divination, such as tarot bags and rune pouches.

Ptah (aka Ptah-Nun, Ptah-Naunet, Khery-Bakef): The Egyptian god of craftsmen. Invoke him for projects that are meant to adorn and beautify.

Sarasvati: The Hindu goddess of knowledge, music, arts, wisdom, and learning. Invoke her for projects meant to enhance learning or meditation.

Seshat: An Egyptian goddess of writing. Invoke her for any projects related to writing, projects related to keeping track of history (embroidered family trees, wedding samplers, growth charts), and also in any record-keeping in relation to arts and crafts businesses.

Uttu: The Mesopotamian/Sumerian goddess of weaving. She is called on for weaving, knitting, crochet, and macramé projects.

Vishwakarma: The Hindu god of artisans and architects. Dedicate your tools to Vishwakarma for excellence in all your crafting endeavors.

Vulcan: The Roman god of fire, metalworking, and the forge. Invoke him for projects involving metal buttons, trims, and fasteners, projects that need an infusion of fire energy, and kitchen projects like pot holders, trivets, and tea cozies.

Wakahirume: The Japanese goddess of weaving. Her symbols are needles, thread, yarn, and embroidered or woven items. Call on her for help with projects involving weaving, embroidery, knitting, crochet, macramé, etc.

Xochipilli: An Aztec god known as "Lord of Flowers" and patron god of poetry, inner vision, and music. Invoke him for help with projects for divination (rune or tarot pouches, divination mats, etc.) or projects that are meant to beautify (the home, self, or others).

HOUSE SPIRITS FROM AROUND THE WORLD

Household spirits that help with chores and protect the home seems to be a Western European belief, specifically Irish, Scottish, English, and Scandinavian. That's not to say there aren't household spirits in other cultures around the world, but rather that those spirits have often been enfolded into a Western definition, shoehorning them into roles that they might not actually fulfill. The duende, for example, from Filipino and Latin American folklore, does share some qualities with brownies, Nisse, and so on in that it is an otherworld creature that may be helpful to mortals or may reside in a home as a household spirit. They play other roles, however, and their overlap with their Western "counterparts" isn't as large as early folklorists might have thought. Similar to how medieval monks recorded Pagan myths and legends with a Christian interpretation, these spirits are reported with an eye to categorizing them in a Western faery taxonomy.

There are, no doubt, other spirits that have domain over the domestic sphere that haven't been co-opted for classification. The list below is offered as a possible starting point for practitioners of non-Western Pagan paths who want to work with house spirits that are not from Irish, Scottish, or Scandinavian cultures.

Aitvaras: A Lithuanian household spirit in the form of bird. It brings good or bad luck and steals gold and grain for the household.

Anito: Used to refer to household deities in the Philippines.

Cofgodas: Evolved from *kofewalt*, "spirit that has power over a room," in Anglo-Saxon Paganism.

Domovoi: A Slavic protective house spirit; it is related to ancestor spirits.

Gashin: Deities believed to protect the various objects and rooms of the house in Korean shamanism.

Jack o' the Bowl: A helpful Swiss house spirit.

Kotihaltia: A Finnish spirit that lives in the attic or barn.

Lares: Roman souls of departed ancestors.

Lutin: A house spirit in France, especially Normandy.

Trasgu: An Asturian house spirit, sometimes helpful, mostly mischievous.

Zashiki-Warashi: Japanese spirits/gods who live in storage rooms, play pranks, and can bring good luck to households.

SLEEP AND DREAM DEITIES

Our time spent asleep can be some of our most magickal, and vulnerable, hours. Deities have often been invoked to guard our sleep, guide our dreams, and to bring us wisdom and messages from our departed loved ones. The list below is a sampling of those from around the world who govern that drowsy domain.

Bormo: The Celtic god associated with secrets revealed through dreaming.

Breksta: The Lithuanian goddess of dreams.

Caer Ibormeith: Irish goddess of sleep.

Epona: The Roman/Celtic horse goddess associated with dreams.

Hypnos: The Greek god of sleep.

Morpheus: The Greek god of dreams.

Muludaianinis: Aboriginal gods of sleep.

Nyx: The Greek god of night.

Olokun: The Yoruban orisha of the deep sea, dreams, and divination.

Phobetor: The Greek personification of nightmares.

COLORS

Use the list of colors and their correspondences when choosing fabrics, thread, pinheads (see page 12), embellishments, and so on to bring their energies into your project.

Color	Correspondences
Black	Absorbing energies, banishing negativity, beginning, binding, death, defense, divination, law, protection, removing discord or confusion, reversing, truth. Especially useful for pouches holding divination tools, altar cloths, binding spells, and poppets.
White	Balance, cleansing, connecting to higher self, consecration, freedom, health, peace, protection, purity, transformation, truth, warding off doubts and fears. Use for pouches holding divination tools, altar cloths, protection charms, bed linens, and ritual clothing.

Color	Correspondences
Red	Action, assertiveness, business deals, combat, conflict, courage, fertility, fire, hunting, passion, power, repairs, self-esteem, sexuality, vigor. Use for purses, pouches for spellwork, bedroom linens (to inspire passion), accessories, and toiletry bags.
Orange	Ambition, breaking down barriers, business success, creativity, harvest, increasing opportunities, intellectual matters, legal matters, pulling things toward you, sealing a spell, strength. Use for kitchen linens and coin purses.
Yellow	Air, beauty, creativity, healing, increase productivity, intellect, inspiration, learning, memory, mental alertness, persuasion, prosperity, remove negative thinking, self-esteem, study, travel. Useful for journal covers, bookmarks, toiletry bags, and book and messenger bags.
Green	Career, changing direction or attitudes, courage, earth, employment, fertility, general healing, growth, luck, money, new beginnings, prosperity. Use for purses and pouches, witch stitches on work clothes, prosperity sachets, and work accessories.
Blue	Charity, dreams, domestic harmony, fidelity, health, increasing wisdom, insight, meditation, patience, peace, removing bad vibrations, self-improvement, water, willpower. Use for toiletry bags, pillowcases and dream pillows, bathroom linens, and meditation cushions.
Purple	Ambition, clairvoyance, change luck, communication, forgiveness, independence, influence, justice, memory, neutralize another's magick, protection, psychic powers, spiritual protection, spirituality, wisdom. Use for meditation pillows, spell pouches, witch stitches on clothes being worn to court, and protective charms.
Silver	Balance, communication, dreams, intuition, meditation, moon magick, psychic awareness, stability, success, ward against negativity. Use in dream pillows, meditation cushions, protective clothing like scarves, and pouches for divination tools.
Gold	Abundance, attraction, health, hope, luxury, mental growth, physical strength, prosperity, success, sun energy, understanding. Use for purses, witch stitches on athletic clothing and sports uniforms, prosperity sachets, and accessories.

Color	Correspondences
Pink	Calmness, compassion, creativity, domestic harmony, friendship, inspiration, love, new relationships, openness, protection of children, relaxation, self-improvement. Use for bedroom linens, for children's blankets and spell pouches, for household linens, and to make witch stitches on gifts to friends and children's clothing.
Brown	Earth, focus, food, fruitfulness, groundings, harvest, house blessing, organization, practicality, security, sound decision-making, stability. Use for kitchen linens, tablecloths and napkins, wallets and purses, and rugs and welcome mats.
Gray	Balance, cancellation, contemplation, dreams, dignity, endurance, neutrality, patience, respect, reversing negativity, stone, travel, veiling. Use in purses, luggage, witch stitches on coats and outdoor wear, dream pillows, and spell pouches.

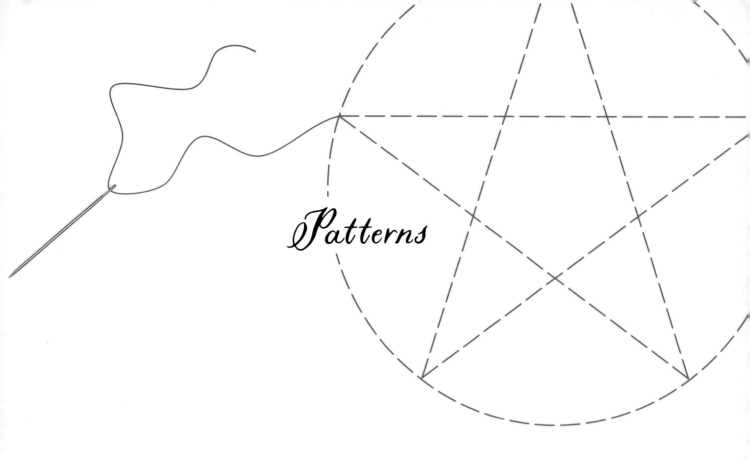

Patterns

his section contains the patterns for the projects on pages 94 through 211. They are printed at 100 percent, so there is no need to enlarge. You can either trace the patterns onto tracing paper or use a photocopier to make copies.

The pieces for the Bias Binding Pentacle Altar Cloth, Sewing Poppet, and Foraging Bag span more than one page. An assembly guide image has been provided to show you how the pieces connect together. If you are using photocopies, cut out the pieces and connect them at the dotted lines with tape. If you are tracing them onto paper, use the dotted lines as a guide to where you should line up the edges.

The charts for the cross stitch projects provided on pages 148 through 150 show what color thread you need for each design. You can, however, substitute any of the suggested colors for ones of your own choosing.

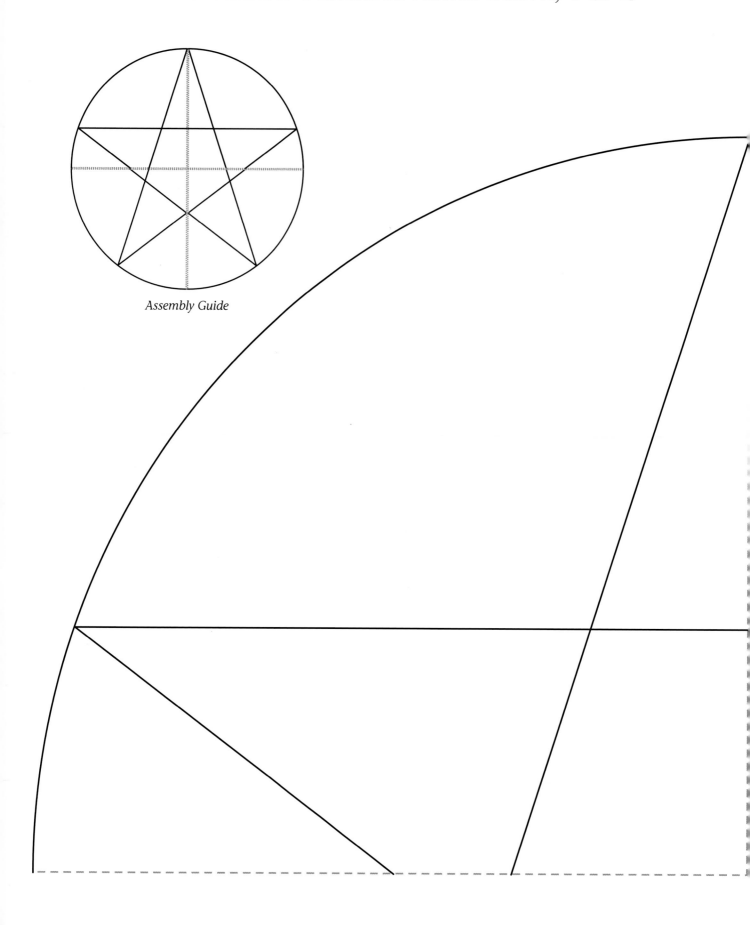

Assembly Guide

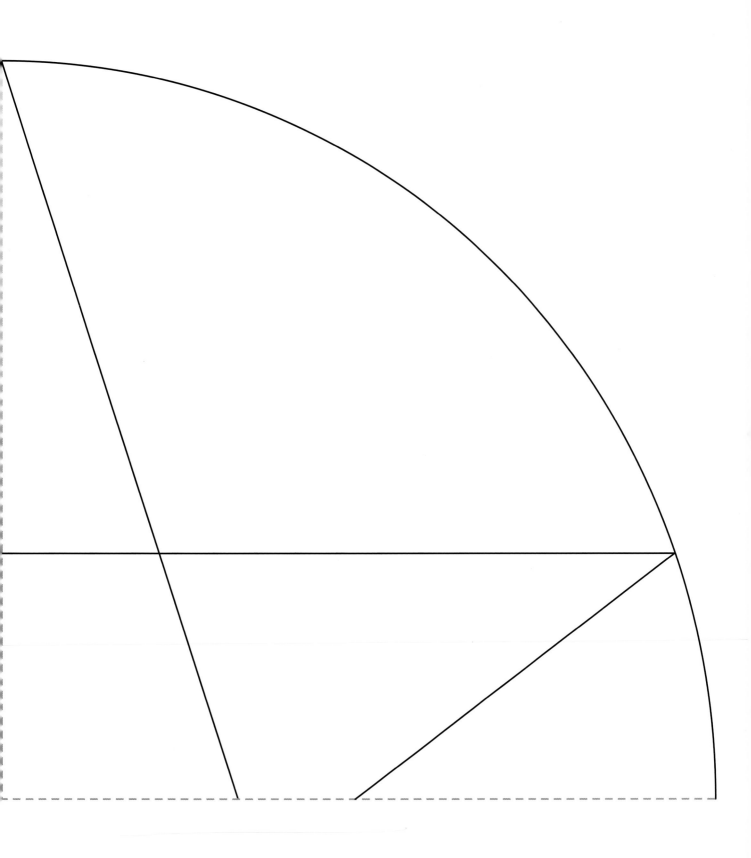

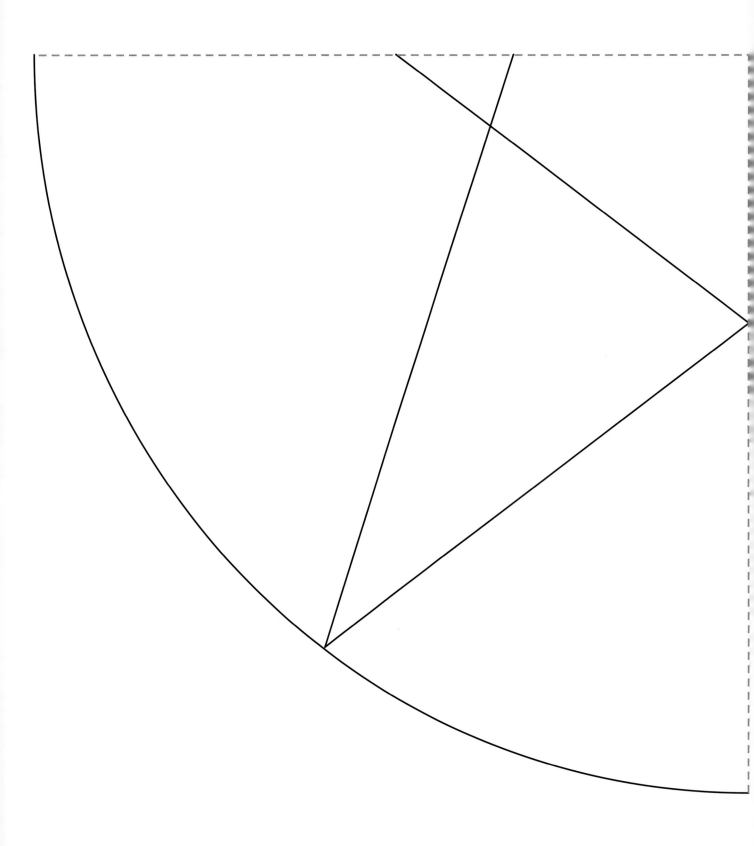

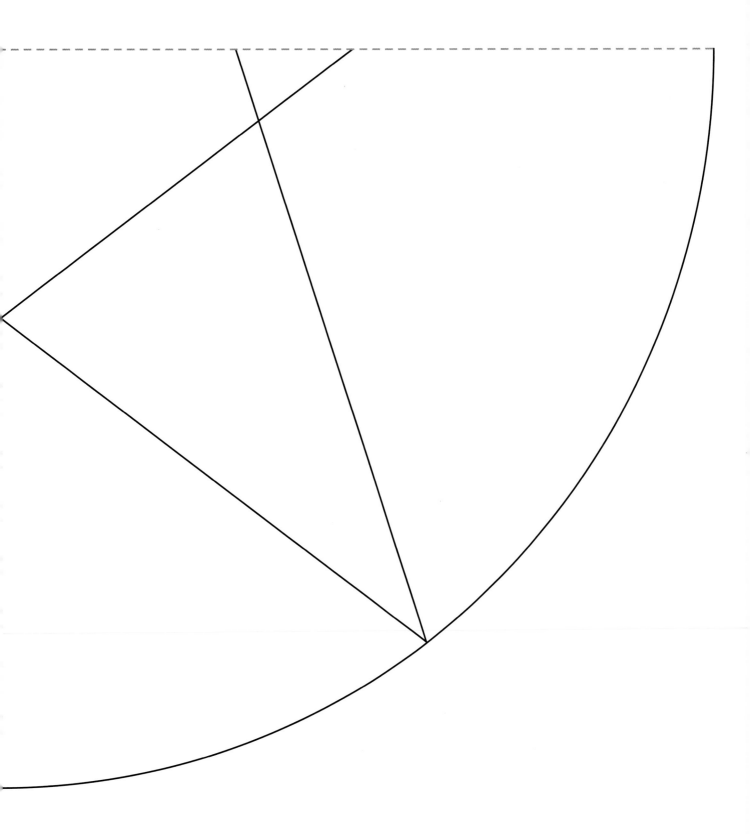

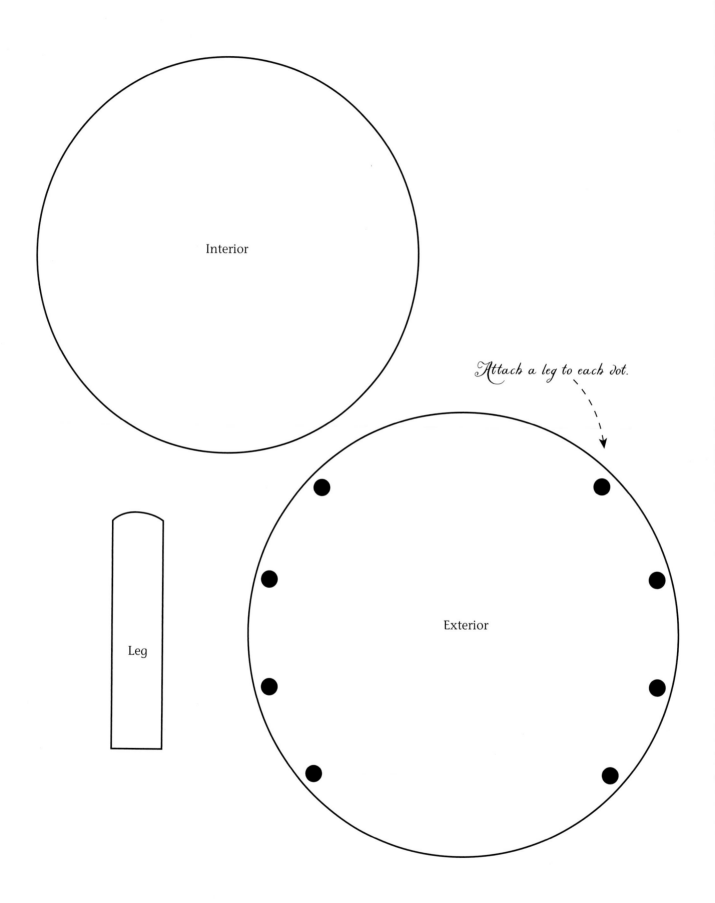

Interior

Attach a leg to each dot.

Leg

Exterior

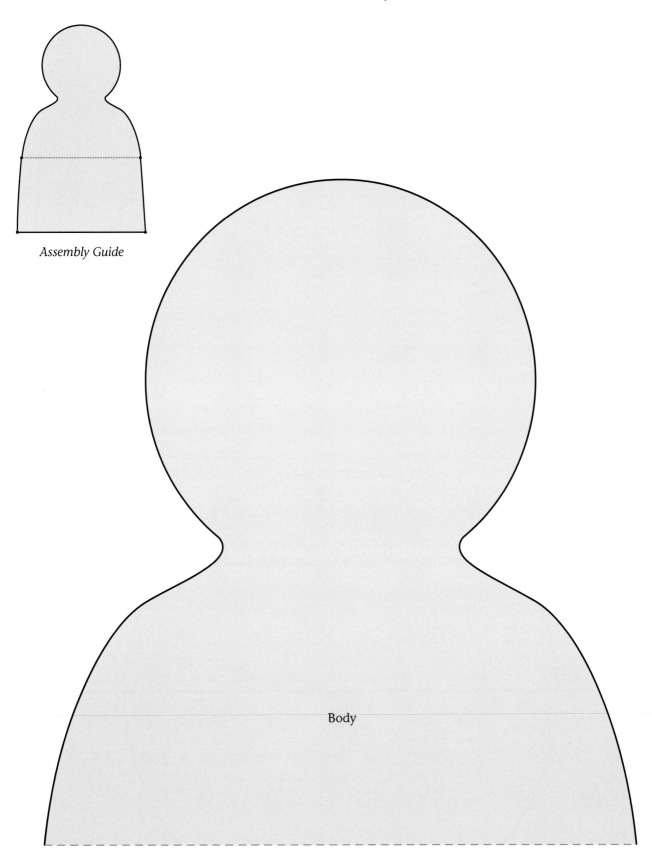

Assembly Guide

Body

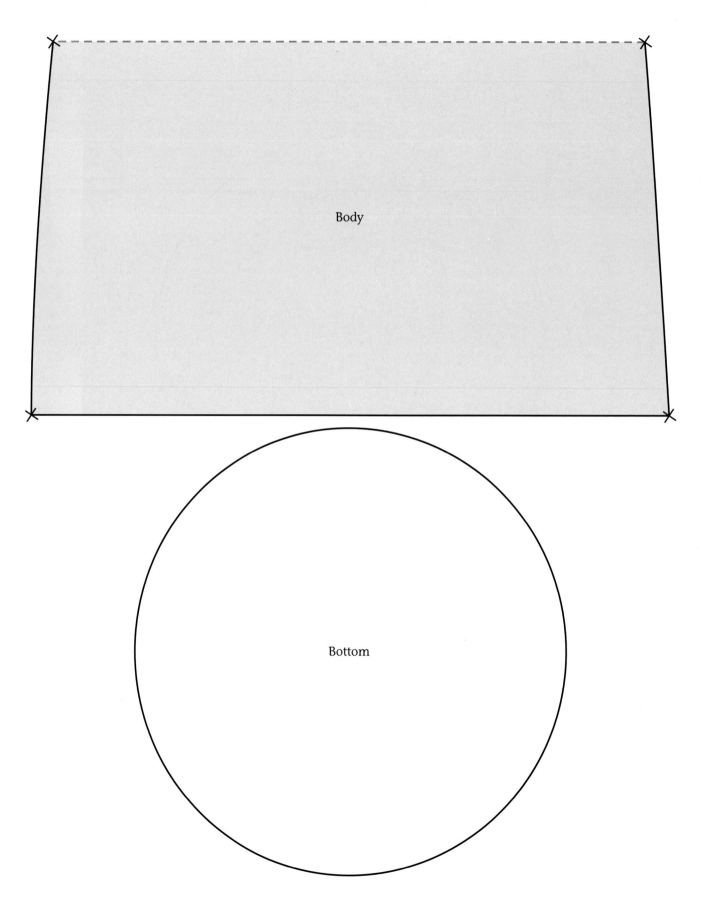

Body

Bottom

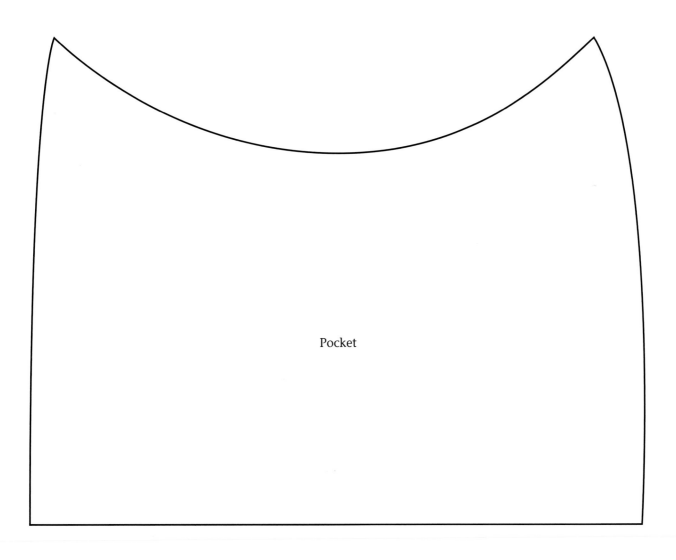

Pocket

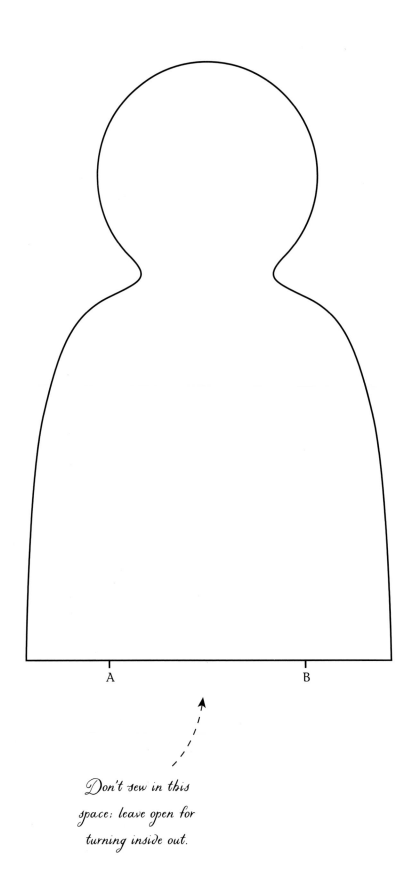

A   B

Don't sew in this space; leave open for turning inside out.

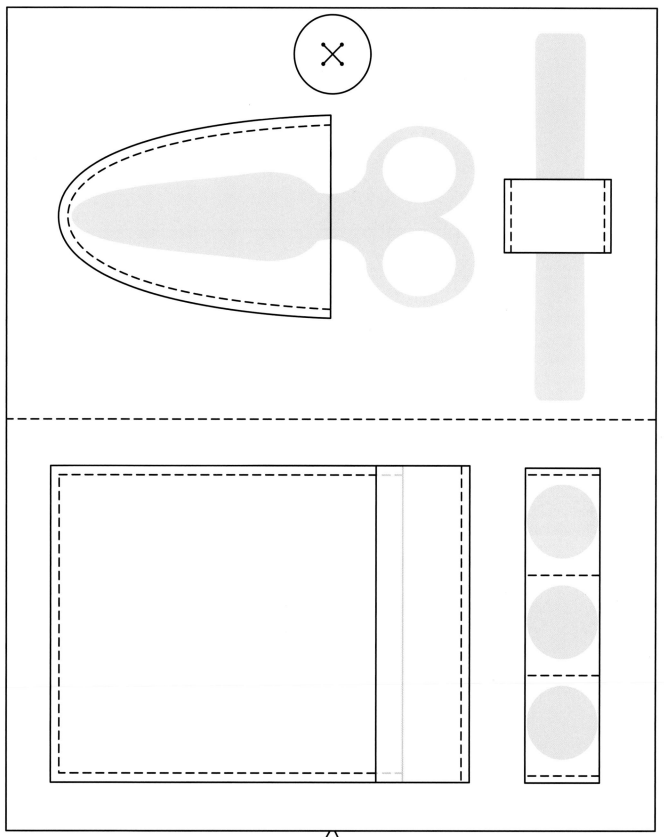

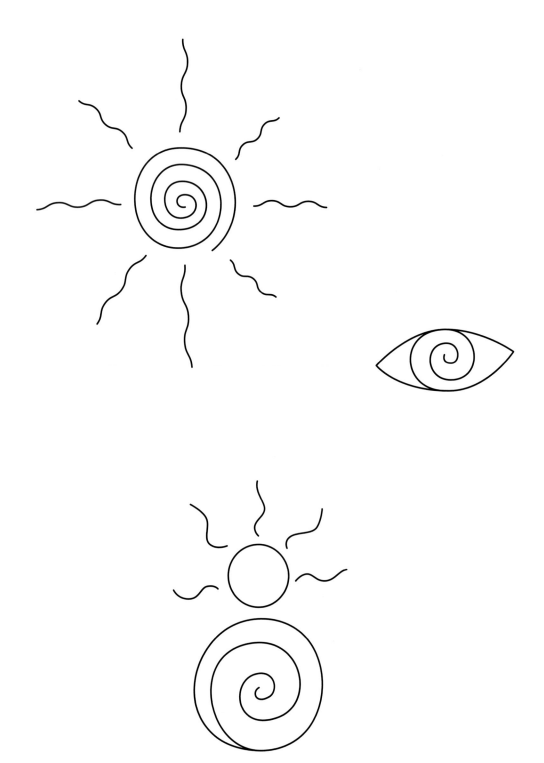

COLORS

- ■ Black
- ■ Green
- ▯ Yellow
- ▯ Coral
- ▯ Pink

Colors

- ⬛ Black
- ▨ Forest Green
- ▨ Yellow
- ▨ Maroon

COLORS

■	Black
■	Gray
▌	Yellow
■	Maroon

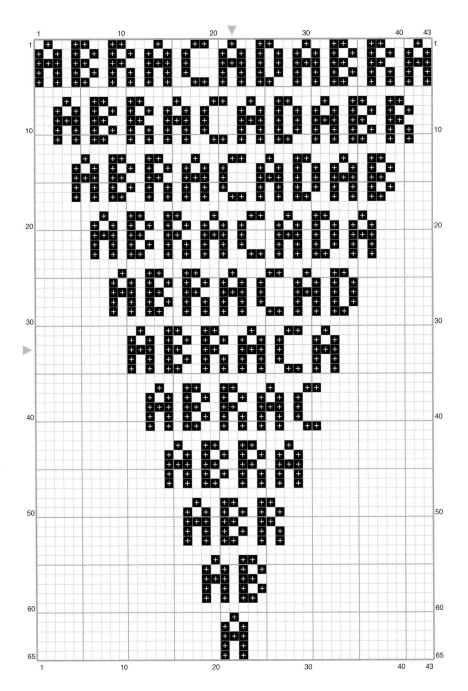

COLOR

■ Black

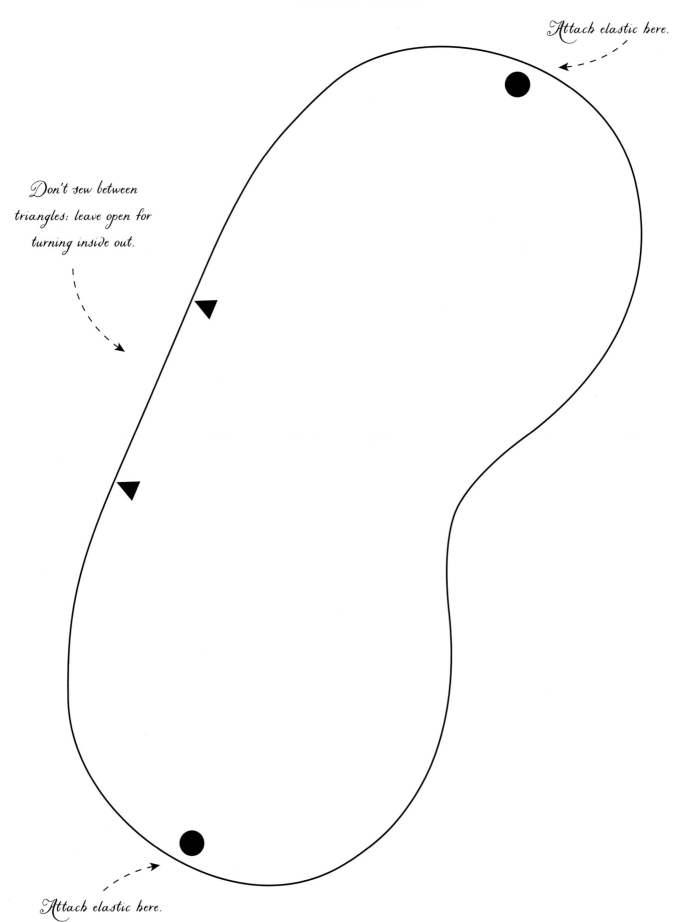

Attach elastic here.

Don't sew between triangles; leave open for turning inside out.

Attach elastic here.

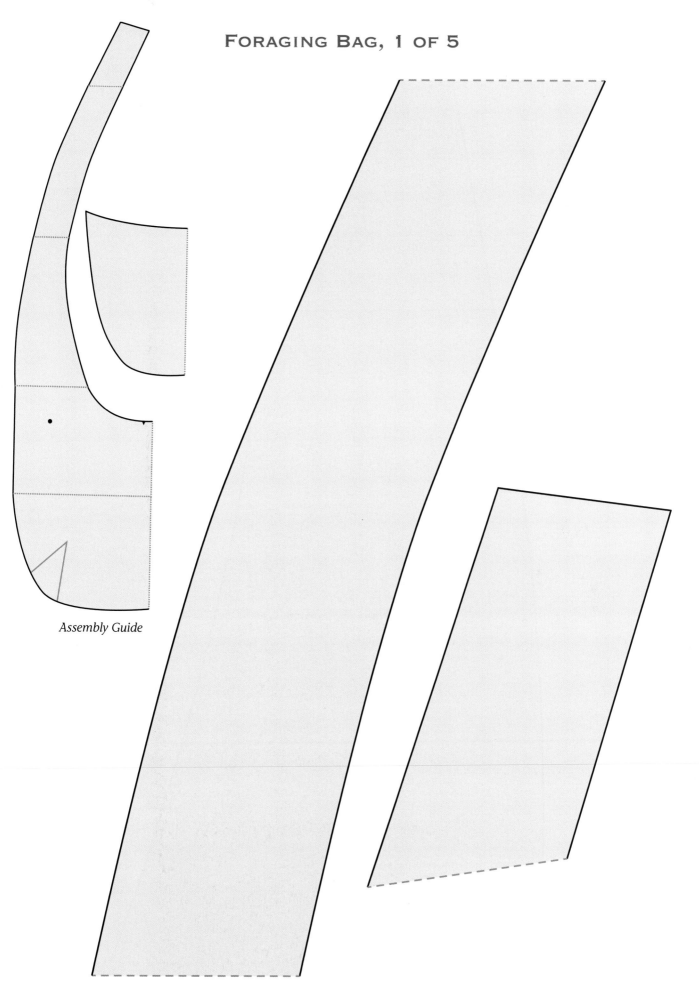

Assembly Guide

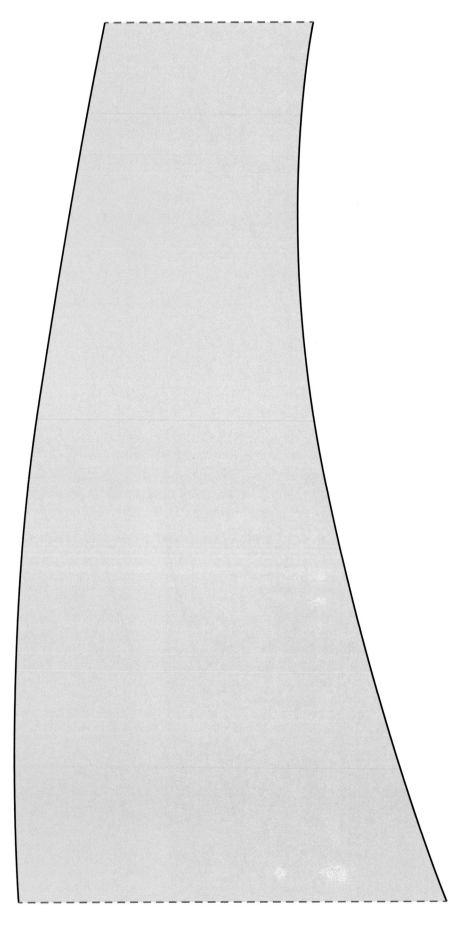

FORAGING BAG, 2 OF 5

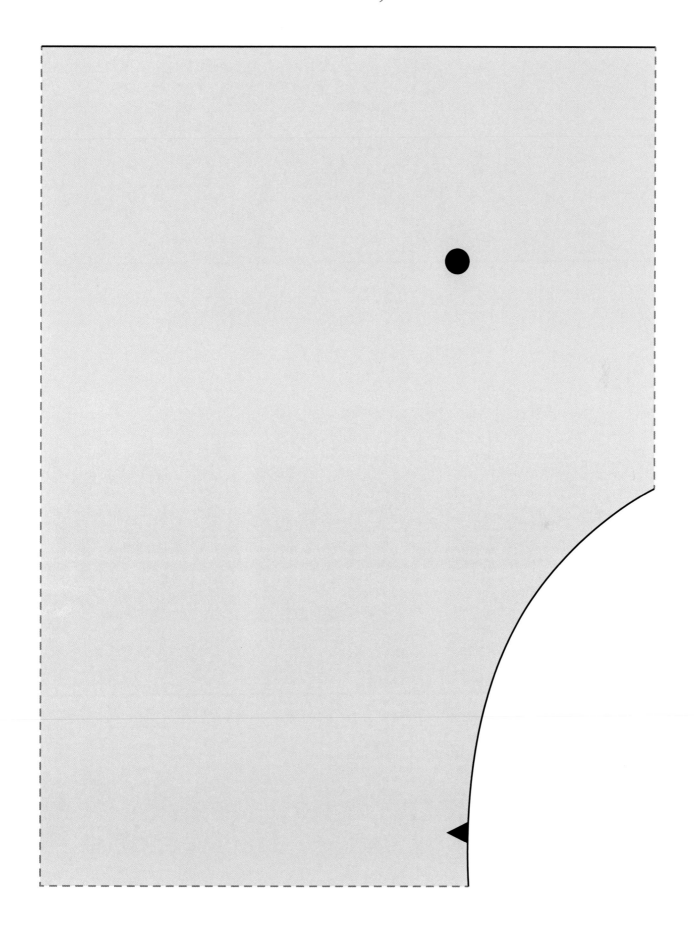

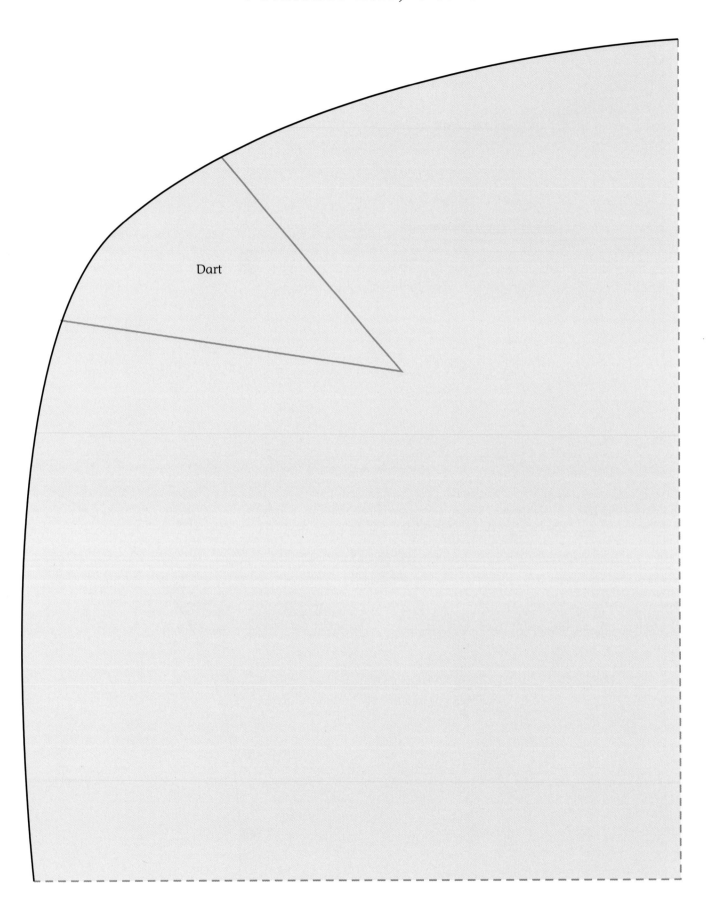

Dart

Pocket

FELT RUNES

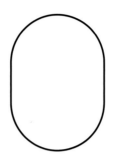

HEART CHARM

SCENTED COASTER (CIRCLE)

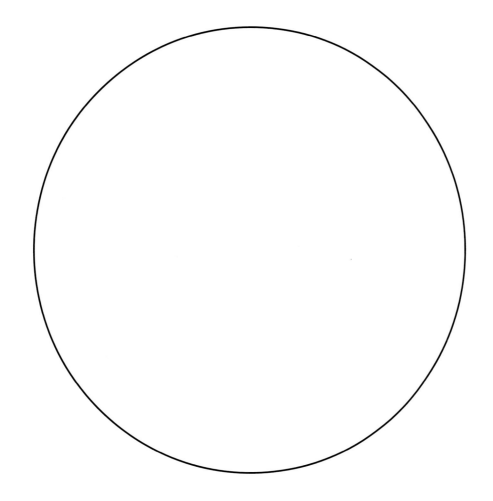

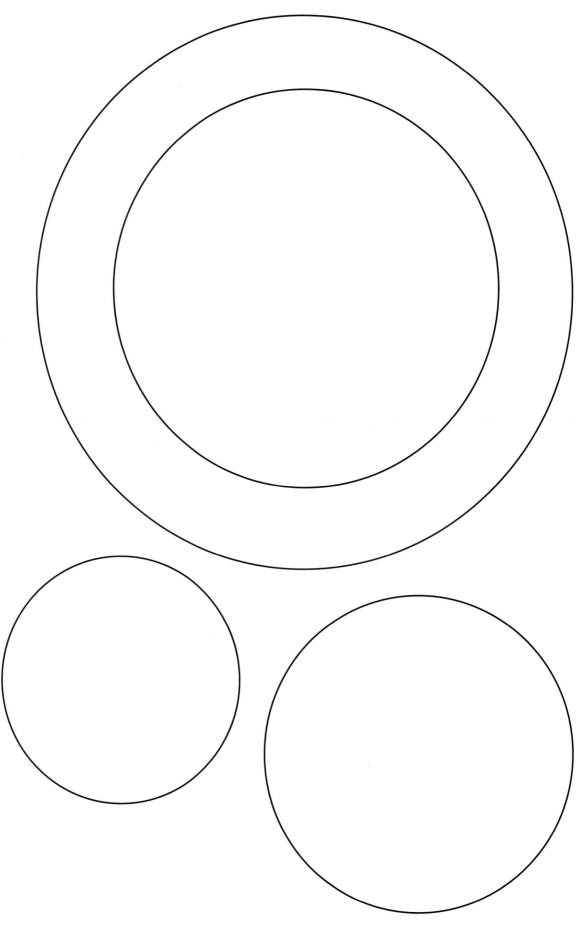

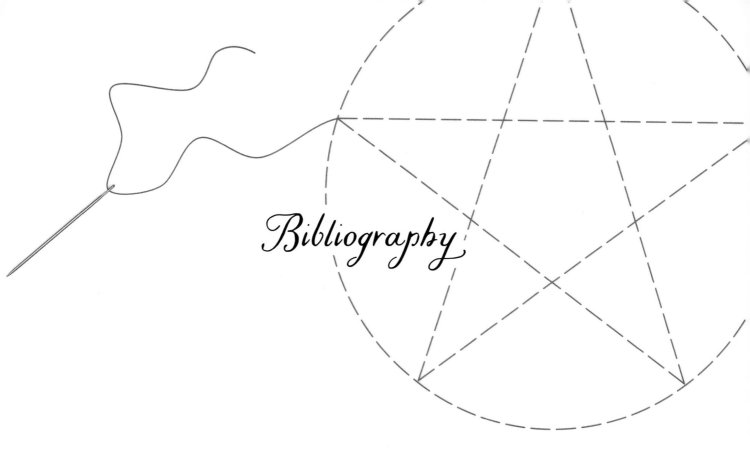

Bibliography

Andrews, J. B. "Neapolitan Witchcraft." Quoted in Grimassi, Raven. *Old World Witchcraft*. San Francisco: Weiser, 2011. Page 73.

Armand, Khi. *Clearing Spaces*. New York: Sterling Ethos, 2017.

Ashmore, Sonia. *Muslin*. London: V & A Publishing, 2012. Page 8.

Beckert, Sven. *Empire of Cotton*. New York: Alfred A. Knopf, 2014. Page 6.

Cooper, D. Jason. *Esoteric Rune Magic: The Elder Futhark in Magic, Astral Projection, and Spiritual Development*. St. Paul, MN: Llewellyn Publications, 1994.

Cunningham, Scott. *Cunningham's Encyclopedia of Magical Herbs*. St. Paul, MN: Llewellyn Publications, 1996. Page 84.

Cunnigham, Scott, and David Harrington. *The Magical Household*. St. Paul, MN: Llewellyn Publications, 1983.

———. *Spell Crafts: Creating Magical Objects*. St. Paul, MN: Llewellyn Publications, 1993.

Eason, Cassandra. *The Magick of Faeries*. Woodbury, MN: Llewellyn Publications, 2013.

Francese, Chris. "Abracadabra (Serenus Sammonicus Lib. Med. 923-941)." Latin Poetry Podcast. May 13, 2013. http://blogs.dickinson.edu/latin-poetry-podcast /2013/05/13/abracadabra-serenus-sammonicus-lib-med-923-941/.

Frazer, James George. *The Golden Bough*. New York: Collier Books, 1963.

Gårdbäck, Johannes Björn. *Trolldom: Spells and Methods of the Norse Folk Magic Tradition*. Forestville, CA: The Yronwode Institution for the Preservation and Popularization of Indigenous Ethnomagicology, 2015.

Gordon, Beverly. *Textiles.* London: Thames & Hudson, 2011. Page 252.

Grossman, Pam. Foreword to *Literary Witches,* by Taisia Kitaiskaia. New York: Seal Press, 2017. Page 7.

Henderson, Sandi. *Sewing Bits and Pieces.* Hoboken, NJ: Wiley, 2010. Page 141.

Illes, Judika. *Encyclopedia of 5,000 Spells.* New York: HarperOne, 2008. Pages 88–89.

Jordan, Michael. *Encyclopedia of Gods.* New York: Facts On File, 1993.

Keightley, Thomas. *The World Guide to Gnomes, Fairies, Elves, and Other Little People.* New York: Gramercy Books, 2000.

Mack, Carol K., and Dinah Mack. *A Field Guide to Demons, Fairies, Fallen Angels, and Other Subversive Spirits.* New York: Owl Books, 1999.

Marquis, Melanie. *A Witch's World of Magick.* Woodbury, MN: Llewellyn Publications, 2014. Page 7.

Moura, Ann. *Green Witchcraft.* Woodbury, MN: Llewellyn Publications, 2002. Page 49.

Parker, Penny. *Farmhouse Witchcraft.* Bloomington, IN: Xlibris, 2014. Page 24.

Pastoureau, Michel. *The Devil's Cloth.* New York: Washington Square Press, 2003. Page 61.

Picken, Mary Brooks. *Singer Sewing Book.* New York: Singer Sewing Machine Co., 1949. Page 3.

RavenWolf, Silver. *HedgeWitch.* St. Paul, MN: Llewellyn Publications, 2008. Page 156.

Richards, Jake. "Needle Magic in Appalachia." *Holy Stones and Iron Bones* (blog), October 27, 2017. https://littlechicagoconjure13.wordpress.com/2017/10/27 /needle-magic-in-appalachia/.

Zakroff, Laura Tempest. *The Witch's Cauldron.* Woodbury, MN: Llewellyn Publications, 2017. Pages 209–10.

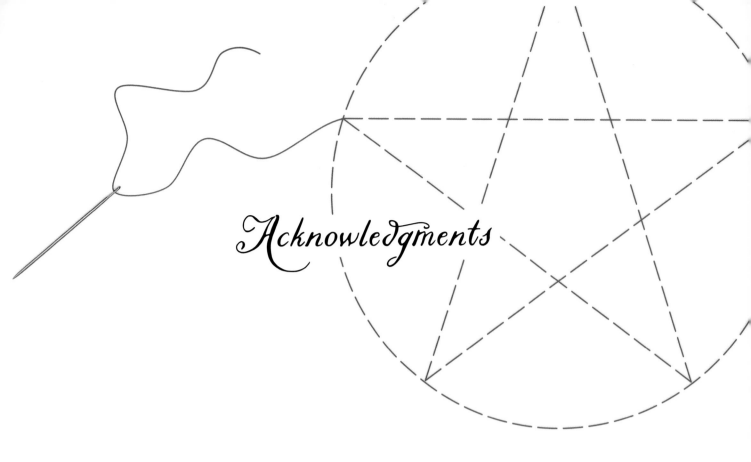

Acknowledgments

This book spent years as just the ghost of an idea in the back of my brain. It might still be there if it weren't for the encouragement and support of the following people:

Stephan, my husband and biggest supporter. He has come along on the journey that has been writing this book from the original spark of inspiration through to the last words.

My crafter-in-crime and booth wife, Moira, has been a source of support for many years. She once said that I make ambitious choices when it comes to my life, and those words have buoyed me through the good and bad times.

The Fountaindale Public Library, specifically the InterLibrary Loan department, helped me gain access to the dozens and dozens of books I read as research. For a time I maxed out the limit of five requests a day, every day, and they didn't bat an eye.

My grandmother, Bonnie Baker. She is a woman of great faith and even greater love for her family. For all my life she has been my role model.

So many friends and family who cheered me on as I wrote, especially Jameson Hogan and Sarah Gullet, who read and commented on portions; Michael Gugerty; and my children, Charlotte and Benjamin, who deigned to be fashion victims . . . erm, models as I drafted the cape and robe patterns in this book. And Trey and Adelia Thoelcke, who opened their home to me to photograph some of the projects in this book.

Finally, my editor at Llewellyn, Elysia Gallo, and the production editor and designer, Lauryn Heineman, helped so much in taking the rough draft of this book and polishing it into the book it is today. It is so much better thanks to their advice and help.

TO WRITE TO THE AUTHOR

If you wish to contact the author or would like more information about this book, please write to the authors in care of Llewellyn Worldwide Ltd. and we will forward your request. Both the authors and the publisher appreciate hearing from you and learning of your enjoyment of this book and how it has helped you. Llewellyn Worldwide Ltd. cannot guarantee that every letter written to the authors can be answered, but all will be forwarded. Please write to:

Raechel Henderson
℅ Llewellyn Worldwide
2143 Wooddale Drive
Woodbury, MN 55125-2989

Please enclose a self-addressed stamped envelope for reply,
or $1.00 to cover costs. If outside the USA, enclose
an international postal reply coupon.

Many of Llewellyn's authors have websites with additional information and resources. For more information, please visit our website at http://www.llewellyn.com.

GET MORE AT LLEWELLYN.COM

Visit us online to browse hundreds of our books and decks, plus sign up to receive our e-newsletters and exclusive online offers.

- Free tarot readings • Spell-a-Day • Moon phases
- Recipes, spells, and tips • Blogs • Encyclopedia
- Author interviews, articles, and upcoming events

GET SOCIAL WITH LLEWELLYN

Find us on  🐦 @LlewellynBooks

www.Facebook.com/LlewellynBooks

GET BOOKS AT LLEWELLYN

LLEWELLYN ORDERING INFORMATION

Order online: Visit our website at www.llewellyn.com to select your books and place an order on our secure server.

Order by phone:
- Call toll free within the US at 1-877-NEW-WRLD (1-877-639-9753)
- We accept VISA, MasterCard, American Express, and Discover.

Order by mail:
Send the full price of your order (MN residents add 6.875% sales tax) in US funds plus postage and handling to: Llewellyn Worldwide, 2143 Wooddale Drive, Woodbury, MN 55125-2989

POSTAGE AND HANDLING

STANDARD (US):(Please allow 12 business days)
$30.00 and under, add $6.00.
$30.01 and over, FREE SHIPPING.

CANADA:
We cannot ship to Canada. Please shop your local bookstore or Amazon Canada.

INTERNATIONAL:
Customers pay the actual shipping cost to the final destination, which includes tracking information.

Visit us online for more shipping options. Prices subject to change.

FREE CATALOG!

To order, call 1-877-NEW-WRLD ext. 8236 or visit our website